D1015516

NORMAN CORWIN'S

ONE WORLD
FLIGHT

The Lost Journal
of Radio's
Greatest Writer

NORMAN CORWIN'S

ONE WORLD
FLIGHT

The Lost Journal
of Radio's
Greatest Writer

edited by Michael C. Keith and Mary Ann Watson

continuum

NEW YORK · LONDON

2009

The Continuum International Publishing Group Inc
80 Maiden Lane, New York, NY 10038

The Continuum International Publishing Group Ltd
The Tower Building, 11 York Road, London SE1 7NX

www.continuumbooks.com

Library of Congress Cataloging-in-Publication Data
A catalog record for this book is available from the Library of Congress

Printed in the United States of America

9780826434111

For my son Anthony, and his paintings.

—N.C.

Contents

IF THIS NOTEBOOK IS LOST
AND FOUND, WILL THE FINDER
PLEASE RETURN IT TO:

NORMAN CORWIN
38 CENTRAL PARK SOUTH,
NEW YORK CITY, 19, N.Y.
U.S.A.

Foreword

The introduction to this book speaks of Norman Corwin as radio's "poet laureate." Twelve years his junior, I've always thought of him as "the patriots' poet laureate." In 1940, having just graduated from high school, my friend Sidney Pasternak and I spent a month traveling through New Hampshire, Maine, and Vermont in our nonpartisan Model T Ford selling Wendell Willkie and Franklin Delano Roosevelt pennants, buttons, and bumper stickers door-to-door, lazing about in between sales on people's lawns and imagining the lives that stretched before us. I knew of Norman Corwin then because I was attracted to "Normans" in public life wherever I might run into them. By the summer of 1940, on relatively short acquaintance, Corwin's words and his poetry had already caught my ear. I remembered that summer and my Willkie pennants so well when, some years later, I read about Norman's One World trip under the auspices of Mr. Willkie. And again, so very many years later when Norman Corwin and I became personal friends. And then later when Norman Cousins moved to California and the three of us referred to ourselves as "The Norman Conquest."

But then, this is about Norman Corwin. I'm sure Norman Cousins, if he were still with us, would agree that Norman Corwin was our peerless leader. He could etch in a few stained-glass words or a metaphor what we might take half a page to say. Corwin's reflections on his One World Flight provide the best example of that. Like the man, they are a compelling blend of characteristics, a combination of marvelously descriptive travelogues, objective foreign reportage, astute political analysis, and profoundly personal reactions to the conditions he finds. Corwin bounces seamlessly from lofty prose to street corner colloquialism and to phraseology

I can only describe as "Corwinesque." His dramatist's sense of pathos and comic timing are here in full measure. The Norman Corwin of 1946 is as staunch a patriot and liberal as the Norman Corwin I know today. In 2001, my wife Lyn and I purchased one of twenty-five extant Dunlop Broadsides, original copies of the U.S. Declaration of Independence printed the night of July 4, 1776, and started a touring exhibition featuring the document. It was axiomatic that I would turn to Norman Corwin to write the essay describing the importance of this document to every living American and the reasons why it was being brought directly to people's hometowns rather than sitting on a wall someplace where they had to travel to find it. Corwin wrote that essay, as he did dozens of other pieces, in words that reveal a deep connection to people of all races and nations; in words that reveal an artist of social conscience who takes endless inspiration from the genius of the American founders.

I'm honored to write this foreword. I stand taller for what Norman Corwin the poet, the patriot, and the person has meant to my life. The best writer to punctuate my message, though, is Corwin himself. "I hope you'll excuse the pretentious comparison," he responded to a reporter asking what he hoped his work would accomplish, "but I think of the *One World Flight* radio series like Pathfinder planes that precede a raid and light up a target. My series may not score a hit, but it might light up the arena that has not hitherto been explored . . . anyway, it will all be up to history, if history is interested."

History is indeed interested, Norman. So is the future.

Norman Lear

Editors' Acknowledgments

Our appreciation to media studies specialist Katie Gallof of the Continuum International Publishing Group is enormous. She welcomed this project with an enthusiastic understanding of its historical, as well as contemporary, significance. Her encouragement, attention to detail, and good humor never waned.

The papers of Norman Corwin housed at the American Radio Archives at the Thousand Oaks Library are in the loving care of Jeanette Berard. She has been remarkably generous with her time and patience. Her thorough knowledge of Corwin's career and her warm willingness to help in any way possible were critical to the completion of this book.

Professor Randal Baier, multimedia and fine arts specialist at the Halle Library at Eastern Michigan University, contributed to the endeavor in his typical gregarious fashion as a technical perfectionist in the preparation of digital files and as a curious intellectual responding to content. Randy's extensive world travel experience coupled with his knowledge of foreign languages made him the ideal associate for sharing ideas and raising important questions. He owns our continuing gratitude.

The research assistance of Corey Kovoch has been tremendously helpful to us in preparing the manuscript. Corey's fascination with Corwin's One World journey and the alacrity with which he performed his assignments confirmed our initial impression that he is a paragon of a college kid. Sara Arthurs, a gifted copy editor with a happy love of language, contributed her talent—and keen eye—to the proofreading of these pages.

Dennis Watson, captivated with geography, world history, art, and culture, was a perfect project partner. He looked forward to reading each chapter as it was completed. His critiques focused on the key issue of whether or not the editing served the original documents well. With his world atlas at hand, Dennis followed the path of Corwin's trip and offered insights that, in every instance, improved our editorial work.

The publications of other media scholars chronicling the career of Norman Corwin were valuable in putting the One World Flight in a larger context. These include *Norman Corwin and Radio: The Golden Years*, by R. LeRoy Bannerman; *Years of the Electric Ear*, an interview by Douglas Bell for the Directors Guild of America Oral History series; and "A Pathfinding Radio Documentary Series: Norman Corwin's *One World Flight*," by Matthew Ehrlich in the fall 2006 issue of *American Journalism*.

Without the many kindnesses of Christian Borjas it would have been impossible to bring the One World ship into port. He is a prince.

As university professors whose careers have been devoted to the history of broadcasting, we could not have undertaken a project more thrilling or fulfilling. Our admiration and affection for Norman Corwin is boundless, as is our gratitude for his friendship.

Mary Ann Watson
Michael C. Keith

Introduction

A towering figure in broadcast history, Norman Corwin has long been known as "radio's poet laureate." His path to that honor began when he was just four years old and would listen to his older brother practice rhymes assigned for school. Little Norman learned them too, and enjoyed reciting them for his family. His parents, Rose and Sam, and his grandparents and aunts and uncles, loved it when he acted out the scenes. At the conclusion of Robert Browning's *Incident of the French Camp*—"Smiling the boy fell dead"—he would throw himself to the floor.

As a schoolboy, his precocious talent for writing was encouraged by his teachers at the U. S. Grant Elementary School in East Boston. Norman wrote full-length stories filled with history and adventure. At Winthrop High, he was terrible in math, but a shining star in the English class of Miss Lucy Drew, where great poets were studied and read aloud.

Before he finished high school, though, Corwin was lured by a career in writing. In 1926, at age seventeen, he accepted a position as a reporter with the small-town *Greenfield Daily Recorder* in Greenfield, Massachusetts. He also became the paper's film critic, writing a column called *Seeing Things in the Dark*. In 1929, Corwin stepped up the journalism ladder with a move to the distinguished *Springfield Republican*—which, despite its name, was an independent publication.

Corwin's introduction to radio work came when the Westinghouse Company, with radio stations in both Boston and Springfield, contacted the *Springfield Republican* about providing airtime for a fifteen-minute nightly newscast at 10:30. The newspaper would provide the news and the reader in exchange for a plug at the end of each broadcast, "This is Norman Corwin of the *Springfield Republican.*"

With the success of the news segment and other radio announcing assignments, Corwin was emboldened to suggest to Springfield station WBZA that consideration should be given to his idea of writing and presenting a program about poetry. He was given the go-ahead, and the resulting series was called *Rhymes and Cadences.*

After an eight-year stint as newspaperman, Corwin took a job in New York City doing public relations work for the Twentieth Century Fox film studio, promoting such stars as Shirley Temple, Don Ameche, Sonja Henie, and Tyrone Power. It wasn't the most satisfying work, but it was pleasant for Corwin in many ways. During the Great Depression he was earning fifty dollars per week, and the required entertaining of clients and potential story sources came with free—and excellent—meals.

The enthrallment of poetry never diminished. One day Corwin phoned New York radio station WQXR and pitched an idea for a program called *Poetic License.* He was asked to come to the studio to audition, and he was offered the 9:15–9:30 p.m. time slot on Tuesdays. Even though there was no salary to go along with the offer, he accepted. And people started listening.

Corwin experimented with techniques of lifting poetry from the printed page to the living dimensions of voice and sound through dramatic interpretation. The program enlisted the interest of the best modern poets in the East; several appeared as on-air guests. Among them were Joseph Auslander, the first poetry consultant to the Library of Congress; sonneteer David Morton; political and social poet Genevieve Taggart; and Alfred Kreymborg, who shared with Corwin a penchant for verse drama. Occasionally Corwin served as a substitute for A. M. Sullivan, the host of *The New Poetry Hour* on the much larger New York radio station WOR.

In the late 1930s, a creative revolution was underway in the medium. What some people still called "the wireless" was maturing from a novelty into an art form. In 1938, William B. Lewis, the legendary vice president of programming at CBS, was home with the flu and happened to hear the impressive presentation of Edgar Lee Masters's *Spoon River Anthology* on *Poetic License*. Within days he interviewed Corwin for the position of radio director for the prestigious dramatic anthology series *Columbia Workshop*. Though his job was directing the scripts of others, it didn't take long for Corwin's gift as a writer to be recognized. Soon the network introduced a new series and took the unprecedented step of acknowledging an author by calling the series *Norman Corwin's Words without Music*.

Corwin joined the ranks of aural provocateurs such as Archibald MacLeish, Arch Oboler, and Orson Welles. The artistic range of the young writer astonished critics. "He writes," said Clifton Fadiman of the *New Yorker*, "as if he were several men." Just a few weeks after the series presented "The Plot to Overthrow Christmas," a whimsical rhyming fantasy that demonstrated Corwin's lambent wit, the public was startled with his vigorous, defiant attack on fascism in the verse drama *They Fly through the Air with the Greatest of Ease*. Corwin's reputation blossomed and he experienced a sudden accession to celebrity.

With the U.S. entry into World War II, Corwin's themes of the magnificence of the common man and common woman touched a responsive chord in the American people. Many of his programs were historical accomplishments. In 1941, Corwin was commissioned to commemorate the 150th anniversary of the ratification of the Bill of Rights. *We Hold These Truths* was broadcast over all four major radio networks and featured a stellar cast, including Jimmy Stewart, Orson Welles, Lionel Barrymore, and President Franklin Delano Roosevelt. The program, aired just a week after the Japanese attack on Pearl Harbor, reached the largest audience ever assembled for a radio drama. Corwin's words, celebrating and elucidating freedom, stiffened the resolve of a country being asked to sacrifice so much to preserve it.

During the war years the radio industry, growing in strength and prominence, helped foster a national spirit of cooperation. Patriotic themes permeated the airwaves—and so did the works of Norman Corwin. One of the most ambitious radio projects of

World War II was the CBS series *An American in England*, which united the talents of Norman Corwin and Edward R. Murrow. The Benjamin Britten score was performed by the London Symphony. The programs—written, produced, and directed by Corwin to promote Anglo-American solidarity—were shortwaved across the United States. Corwin's prolific output of quality during this period was a key factor in the prestige image enjoyed by the CBS network for years to come.

In the late summer of 1943 a new Corwin series, *Passport for Adams*, starred Robert Young as a small-town newspaper editor on a goodwill mission to countries favoring the Allied cause. In the spring of 1944, with *Columbia Presents Corwin*, the young man from Boston continued to earn the accolades of critics and to be regarded by the public as radio's big gun.

Toward the end of 1944, with an Allied victory in Europe apparently assured, CBS asked Corwin to prepare a program celebrating the anticipated event. On May 8, 1945, just after the collapse of Germany, CBS aired *On a Note of Triumph*, an epic aural mosaic. This program is considered to be the climax of the luminous period in radio history when writing of high merit, produced with consummate skill, was nurtured—as well as protected from commercial interference.

After the broadcast, phone calls and letters of praise flooded the network, including a letter from Carl Sandburg calling *On a Note of Triumph* "one of the all-time great American poems." The script of the program in book form, released by Simon and Schuster, sold out so quickly that the publisher rushed a second printing the following week.

Many honors were showered upon Norman in the months following the end of the war. In 1946, a particularly significant one was reported in *Time* magazine:

> Norman Corwin, radio's 35-year-old wonder-boy enjoyed a week befitting his prestige. He won the first Wendell Willkie Award— a trip around the world sponsored by Freedom House and the Common Council for American Unity. Skipping lightly over all

other U.S. writers and artists, the organization thought Corwin's *On a Note of Triumph* was the best contribution to the concept of One World in the field of mass communication.

Wendell Willkie ran for president as the Republican opponent to Roosevelt in 1940. In his early years as a young lawyer he had been a liberal Democrat. But after becoming wealthy in a successful corporate legal practice he became the head of a public utility company and was opposed to the New Deal creation of the Tennessee Valley Authority, which competed with his company. His financial conservatism did not dim his liberal social views, however. In 1941, together with Eleanor Roosevelt, he helped establish Freedom House, a bipartisan organization dedicated to democracy and human rights.

In 1942, Willkie was appointed by President Roosevelt to serve as his personal ambassador at large. His mission was to go around a world still in the throes of war to meet with the Allies. On his fifty-day trip in 1942, Willkie reinforced America's commitment to the defeat of fascism. Upon his return, he wrote *One World,* a best-selling plea for international cooperation after the war.

Willkie attempted to move the Republican Party to a more liberal and progressive stance by seeking the presidential nomination again in 1944. But his strong advocacy of civil rights and the Social Security program precluded him from being the nominee. Tragically, Willkie died of a heart attack in the summer of 1944 at the age of fifty-two. Friends of Willkie created a living memorial by establishing the One World Award, a subsidized around-the-globe trip in the mold of his historic 1942 mission. No more ideal candidate for the prize could be found than its first recipient.

The story of Norman Corwin's One World Flight is told in his voice in the chapters of this book. Each chapter is derived from a blend of sources, primarily the handwritten journal that Corwin kept throughout his four months of travel and a book manuscript based on his journal. The manuscript remained unfinished because work in motion pictures pushed the project off his front burner. New projects arose and decades passed. More than sixty years after his trip, at the urging of this book's editors, a search for the journal and the manuscript ended with the happy result of a distilled document that allows Norman Corwin's thoughts, presented in his rich prose, to be preserved for future generations.

One Way Ticket
New York to New York

There was quite a throng to see us off —

Jacques Ferrand gargled his r's more than the average Frenchman, and held a cigarette in his mouth all the while he talked.
But it was worth listening to him because he had a quiet fervor to
go with his intelligent eyes and canny nose, and an irrepressible
good will. Peace was his hobby, and he worked hard at it. He was
forever promoting good causes and dragging me into them. I had
to be dragged not because of indifference but because there were
programs to get out, and I lacked time.

Ferrand was always bringing people together for what show-
biz half-affectionately calls clambakes. He was executive secretary
for an organization awkwardly named The Common Council
for American Unity, and also, at one time or another, possibly
simultaneously, he held the same office for the American Nobel
Prize Committee and the One World Award Committee. Also he
had diplomatic relations with Freedom House and The Wendell
Willkie Memorial Foundation. Exactly how these groups inter-
related I never knew. It was less trouble to yield to Ferrand's per-
sistent coaxing to speak at this or that function, than to figure out
which was which and what for.

In any case it was in his role as do-gooder for the One World
Award Committee, that Ferrand approached me one day early in

1946, and asked me if I would accept an award which would mean flying around the world, roughly along the path taken by Wendell Willkie four years earlier, during the war, when he went at the bidding of President Roosevelt to visit our allies, see how they were doing, and urge them on.

Willkie returned from that trip, wrote an enormous best seller by the title of *One World*, and transformed himself from a dyed-in-the-wool, deep-fried conservative, into a liberal in free orbit, off to the left of many a Democrat. As the country well knows, he died untimely in 1944, leaving a cavernous vacuum in liberal Republican ranks.

To perpetuate his memory, a group of his friends and admirers established the One World Award. The Awards Committee was motley and crossed party and professional lines, including as it did Senators Fulbright, Kilgore and Pepper, Abel Green of *Variety*, broadcaster Edgar Kobak, singer Benay Venuta, Walter White, Chief Secretary of the NAACP, Darryl F. Zanuck, former New York governor and banker Herbert H. Lehman, sculptor Jo Davidson, scientist Waldemar Kaempffert, and Congressmen Sal Bloom and Adolph J. Sabath. *The New York Herald Tribune*, through its publisher, Mrs. Ogden Reid, was a friend of the project, and so was Pan American Airways.

I told Ferrand I would accept the award only if it could be a working trip, and if I could bring back material for a series of at least thirteen broadcasts. Also there was CBS to be reckoned with, since I was under contract to them. If network head Bill Paley declined to let me go, or had urgent work for me, or did not care to contribute the network's resources to help keep green the memory of Willkie, I would of course respect my contract and pass up the award; and I made it clear that I would not try to persuade him. Paley's consent would have to come unprompted.

It did. He consented with the panache of a Medici, and vice-president Davidson Taylor wrote a letter to Freedom House saying CBS was "proud" and would cooperate. But every do-good prospect has a price, whether it be to raise a statue to Stan Musial or help indigent vaqueros on the pampas. After the first flush of committee concord comes the matter of raising money, and that is a bore and a grind to the raisers.

Ferrand always began by thinking big, and irised down as necessary. At first he spoke of a special plane, which was the way Willkie traveled. But Willkie was sent by the United States Government, which, unlike Ferrand and friends, had a great many planes at its disposal. Somehow Howard Hughes, who at that time was thought to have citizenly impulses toward national and world affairs, came up in the discussions, but nobody ever broached to him the idea of furnishing an airplane. I was glad of that, for a private ship would have been the wrong way for a radioman to get about, and would have placed the mission under an obligation to be grand.

At length the funding aspects of the Flight, from all of which I scrupulously stayed clear, were worked out. I knew only that CBS was underwriting the cost of sending an aide along, and that the trip was scheduled to begin on June 15, 1946.

I was offered my pick of the CBS production staff to accompany me on the trip, and nominated Lee Bland, who had given me a strong assist on "Stars In The Afternoon" at Carnegie Hall. On that occasion I had written a paean-type memo to his superior, and now, remembering his services under fire, his resourcefulness, diplomacy and energy, I figured they might come in handy on a long haul.

On the 54th anniversary of Willkie's birth, the award was announced at a black-tie dinner on the Starlight Roof of the Waldorf Astoria. Present, in one of the last stands of undismayed liberalism before McCarthyism fell on the land, were the ranking Willkie-minded people of the city and the day. On the dais were Willkie's widow and his son Philip. I sat between young Willkie and Fiorello LaGuardia; further along were Walter Lippmann, Chief Justice of the Supreme Court Charles Evans Hughes, Jr., 20th Century Fox President Spyros Skoaras, Helen Hayes, Brooklyn College President Marquis Childs, Dr. Harry Gideonse, Walter White, and the Attorney General of New York, Nathan Goldstein. There was a good tone to the evening, restrained speechmaking, no bad jokes, no attempts to reform the world, nothing windy or overlong.

Walter Lippmann said of Willkie:

> He was a Republican, and, in his convictions about property and competition and private initiative, a conservative. But he never got into a groove and stayed there. And while he knew the difference between conservatism and radicalism, he never forgot that the difference between right and wrong is more important than the difference between right and left.

Mayor LaGuardia, presenting the award to me, said he hoped a national memorial committee would be established to insure perpetuation of the award annually. Accepting, I said that Willkie's concept had on its side

> the virtue, in a world not distinguished for cool reasoning, of being logical. When its logic and truth are translated, absorbed, shared and implemented by all people, then his world will come fruitfully about. Then we can talk sensibly about the abundant life. In the meantime, by the instrument of the high honor and responsibility which you entrust to me and to those who will succeed me, you are seeing to it that Willkie's concept circles the earth in a kind of annual orbit.

It was not the last occasion with a meal and speeches, before I took off. But it was still weeks before departure, and preparation for the trip was a hulking labor. Between Bland and myself sixty visas had to be obtained and a program had to be arranged so that in each country, in the few days of our visit, I could use my time to the fullest advantage.

There was much help. Letters went out from CBS Executive Ted Church to network correspondents abroad; from Ferrand to foreign radio systems, civic and governmental bodies, and from the U.S. State Department to its public affairs officers around the world, asking them to give a hand to the visiting missionaries. Bland consulted with CBS engineers and they decided on the equipment to carry: a magnetic wire recorder, a step-down transformer, a 12-volt converter, test meters, a kit of tools, spools of recording wire, miscellaneous cables, plugs and connectors all carried in a big wooden box, the whole weighing 200 pounds. We were just a year too early for tape—a pity, since the wire recorder was heavy, awkward, poor in sound quality, and fickle in performance. It turned out to be Bland's nightmare. He took a cram-course in its peculiarities, but the machine defied understanding and balked with an almost intelligent perverseness.

Visas piled up. Two countries asked irregular questions in their application forms, Sweden wanting to know the applicant's race and religion, and the USSR wanting to know what political parties one had belonged to. To the question on race I replied "Human"; to religion, "Monotheism." I was strongly tempted to make another "none of your business" reply to the Russians but I could not afford to risk losing the visa by offending them on a point of their peculiar xenophobia, because the whole *raison d'etre* of a One World Flight was to visit *both* existing worlds. Without Russia, the trip would have been a travesty on Willkie's objective. One might bypass Sweden, as Willkie did, but not the Russians. So I answered, truthfully enough, "Republican and Democratic," and hoped there would be no further questions of that sort anywhere else around the circuit. There were not.

The preparatory work was demanding, and so were certain social obligations. In Beverly Hills, around this time, admirers of Willkie produced a banquet in the old Florentine Room of the Beverly Wilshire Hotel, at which 500 film and radio people sat around tables to eat the usual roast beef and listen to a program staged by actors, technicians and others whom I had managed not to offend in nine years of broadcasting.

Robert Young was master of ceremonies, and there were readings of excerpts from some of my shows. Edward G. Robinson, Ona Munson, Dane Clark, Alfred Drake, Keenan Wynn, Martin Gabel, Joan Loring, Charles Laughton, each performed a selection from a published script, ranging in subject from the retribution of Bomber Number 6 in *They Fly Through the Air* to the apotheosis that concluded *On A Note Of Triumph*. I sat there hearing myself lionized and praised and quoted as though I had been dead for a generation, or was running for office, and I had to put on a face that showed appreciation and a reasonable modesty and, at the same time concealed doubts about myself and whether I would make the crackerjack world missioner they all were insisting I was. Then Robert Young introduced Paul Robeson, who in his rich basso presented me with "a message of good will" from show people in America, to their colleagues abroad, which follows here:

Like a great many members of our profession, I have traveled during these past few years to appear before the armed forces of my country and before the people of the United Nations. I have lived in some of these European countries at various periods in my life. I have seen fascism. I have witnessed its brutality. I have seen the meaning of bigotry in terms of human life. I have seen it, I am sorry to say, in my own country as well. But I have also seen the victory of the armies and the peoples of the United Nations.

True, it is easier to kill men than ideas. Great ideas, like liberty, like democracy, like freedom of expression, freedom of religion, cannot be crushed. Those who fight and those who die in this battle are succeeded by others who with equal courage and vigor take up the banners and march to final triumph. But, by the same rule, though Hitler and Mussolini are dead, and their armies are defeated, the poison of hate is still being sold, or given away free, by those who bitterly opposed the ideals of Wendell Willkie and Franklin Roosevelt; by those who are afraid of the bright, shining sun of the great tomorrow. But there are those who believe actively in the high purposes for which these two men, Willkie and Roosevelt, lived and died. I have seen the anguished and the suffering; and I have seen the determined, the bold and the brave who have withstood the tyrants of Europe and I see the same democratic determination here tonight.

The great mass of the people are often times inarticulate. They cannot come to this microphone; their dreams are silent and their lives are sometimes lonely. They wait, in their homes and in their fields and factories, for the voice of a friend; they huddle closely waiting for the word. They have found the voice and the word in Norman Corwin.

Through you, the people have had the opportunity of understanding the events of the world. All success, I have found, is ultimately in the approval of the people. You have reached them through this wonderful invention of radio. And for this you have been honored. And you have honored us because you have brought radio to a higher level of achievement than it has ever reached before. You have had a profound effect on your audiences and you have had a deep and abiding effect on our standards—and I mean those of us who have appeared on your programs.

Now you are about to embark on a trip around the world, the one world. You will meet the peoples of the United Nations. It is my privilege, in the name of the people assembled here, to present to you, Norman Corwin, a message to the peoples of the United Nations.

It was then my turn, and in passing I paid respects to the medium, which was even then broadcasting the occasion over the Pacific network of CBS:

I consider myself a product of a system of radio, which, for all its faults, and some of them are grievous, is perhaps the freest in the world. I wish I could say that was true all of the time of all of the stations. It is not. But whatever indictments may be brought against American radio, it manages, on the network level, to give a measure of both sides of any controversial issue, which certainly is more than can be said of great areas of the press.

Later, after suggesting that Madison Avenue energies and techniques might well be turned to the selling of Democracy as well as Wheaties, I attempted to define partisanship and politics:

There are those who want to change nothing about anything; not even if the status quo means unfair employment practices, floods in the Missouri valley, inflation, ten million jobless, and the traditional cycle of intermittent wars. They are one side. The so-called progressive is on the other. But there is a third category. I don't mean the fence-sitter who leans one way and then the other, under the impression he is on both sides, when actually he is on neither. At least the fence-sitter knows there is such a thing as a fence. The man I mean just floats in air, like a prop in an Indian rope trick. He tells you he is not interested in politics; that he just wants to go along peacefully minding his own or his company's business or his art, and not go mixing in politics.

I'll tell you what politics is. It's your bank account and the assets of your corporation, and the freedom of your art; it's the roof over your head, and whether it needs repair from bomb damage; it's the condition of the roads you ride on, and the quality of the teachers in your schools; the clothes you wear, and whether they are available and reasonably priced. Like it or not, you are the creature of politics and of society; certificates are issued for your birth, vaccination, education, marriage, and death.

Politics is intimate, not a pageant in a remote marble capital; it has to do with the lives and safety of your family and yourself; with whether you can afford to marry; or, if you are married, whether you can afford children. Politics is in the instrument, which determines not only whether the cows, which furnish your milk, are free of tuberculosis, and if there shall be benches in the park, but whether your son will have to die on a battlefield, or whether you yourself will vaporize in a blast of improved nuclear fission.

The man who never takes sides, who never votes, never signs a petition, never speaks his mind, is a civic drone. Panics, depressions and wars come to him like weather. He suddenly peers out of his window and says, "Look, it's warring."

And I went on for another twenty minutes.

It was one of those occasions when an audience, disposed to be friendly and sympathetic to one's point of view, rose to its feet when I finished, to applaud. I was moved, naturally, as who wouldn't be on seeing people get to their feet like that. (I am even touched when anybody gets up from a chair to be introduced—it's a dear old amenity, like tipping one's hat to a lady.) But these were my peers and better, extravagantly better in many instances, for among that audience were artists whose work I had long admired and in some cases revered. Through that ovation (I shall have to call it that since it went on for a couple of minutes), it was good to feel useful and wanted and approved. But when the guests went home, and I too, my small triumph became very little indeed, for there was none to share it with. I was without a girl at that time, between attachments; there had been a long hiatus. And a man is never so much alone as when he faces either victory or defeat without a woman to round off the one or soften the other.

Back to New York I went, and found myself quickly saddled with chairmanship of a dinner honoring the Big Five's chief delegates to the Security Council of the United Nations. It was arranged by the Independent Citizen's Committee of the Arts, Sciences and Professions (ICCASP), at the request of the State Department. It was held at the Astor Roof on the first anniversary of the founding of the UN at San Francisco. It developed that mine was no tranquil chair. So much happened behind the starched shirtfronts that I never got to eat the $12.50 dinner, nor even to talk to Harold Ickes, then Executive Secretary of ICCASP, who sat at my left, or to General George Kenny, who sat at my right.

The first problem was that Andrei Gromyko, the Soviet Union's representative to the UN Security Council, who was scheduled to speak along with Ickes, diplomat Sir Alexander Cadogan of Britain, Ambassador Henri Bonnet of France, UN representative Dr. Thi-Chi Quo of Nationalist China, and Trygve Lie, Secretary General of the UN, announced on arriving that he would *not* speak. Reasons unstated. This set off a series of whispered conferences among and behind people sitting at the head table, while the din of 600 diners filled the room. The Gromyko impasse was finally broken, I know not how, and he did speak.

Then word came to me that Trygve Lie was deeply annoyed, as he had a right to be, because Ickes had impulsively spoken out of turn in the program, a twist which meant that in the order of events, Lie would not be heard in the portion of the program that was to be broadcast. I concurred with Lie, because it had been his understanding that he *would* be part of the radio transmission. But the printed dinner program, distributed to each table, said very clearly that he was one of the speakers, and his large presence was obvious to everybody in the room.

It would have been scandalous if, at a dinner produced to generate good will for the United Nations organization, its highest-ranking official balked from speaking. I got up from my chair, crossed to Lie, and asked him to reconsider. I apologized for Ickes, said his action was inadvertent, and suggested affably that if Lie declined to speak, it would be analogous to a delegation walking out of the General Assembly over some point of protocol. But Lie shook his head vigorously and kept saying, "No, no, no!" to the bewilderment of Lana Turner, who happened to be sitting next to him. She was there, I supposed, representing American culture and beauty.

I returned to my seat, waited until Lie was due on the program, and, as though he had never spoken a word of protest, I barged ahead and introduced him with the esteem to which he was entitled. When I finished he hesitated for a moment, but as applause for him spread across the room and kept building, he smiled, got up, came to the podium, and gave the best speech of the evening.

There were three items of "entertainment" on the program: a reading by Sam Jaffe of E. B. White's "Memorandum to a U.N. Delegate," which had recently run in the *New Yorker*; the singing of a song called "It's Smart To Be People," the lyrics of which had been composed by E. Y. Harburg; and a reading by Art Carney of a piece I had written spoofing Hans Van Kaltenborn's staccato style of political commentary and delivery.

After that evening, there was only one public occasion left before takeoff and that was a farewell luncheon jointly hosted by the Willkie Memorial, the Common Council for American Unity, and CBS, in the Jade Room of the Waldorf. It, too, was broadcast.

Sumner Welles was to have been chairman of the luncheon, but illness kept him home, and Mrs. Ogden Reid took over with her usual sharp diligence.

Herbert Bayard Swope, representing the Willkie Memorial of Freedom House, starting off with sweeping charm, spoke of the projected flight:

> The itinerary is predicated upon a theory that One World is existent. The recipient of the award will be able to tell us how far idealism has been translated into practice. He starts out by flying. Let us hope he won't end by walking. If he is unable to pierce the several iron curtains that exist still throughout the world, it will not be an evidence of failure, but of the pressing need for greater effort on all our parts.

Among the generosities concerning myself, he placed me in the same boat with two celebrities—bailing water:

> Corwin's stuff entitles him to a rank with—but after—two other great Americans, Thomas Paine and Wendell Willkie. Both agreed in the definition of the nationality that would best be suited to the needs of the world when Paine phrased it, "Where freedom is not, there is my country." That I think has been true of the man we are dispatching upon this message of idealism.

Mrs. Reid then introduced William S. Paley, who was paying for the recording hardware and Bland's seat, and the series of broadcasts that would come out of the trip. She praised him for having made CBS internationally minded: "From quite a long ways back Mr. Paley saw into the future with great judgment and clear thinking, and his staff of experts, such as Ed Murrow and Bill Shirer, have brought something of immeasurable value to our own country and also to other countries."

Paley spoke with charm and urbanity, a civilized and hopeful speech:

> I am very happy that after his return Norman will do a series of broadcasts over the Columbia Broadcasting System about his trip around the world. Never before has his mastery of our

medium or his great talent as a writer and producer of radio programs been put to a more important task, and, Norman, as you travel around the world, I hope you will encourage the Wendell Willkies and the Norman Corwins of other lands to make similar trips and to assume similar obligations. It will only be when the peoples of all countries really understand each other that we may have a chance of seeing our One World dream come true, for then, with their bond of understanding and their reliance upon each other, will they have the faith and the courage to stand up, to demand and to get the peace and the security and the opportunity for happiness that they all so desperately want.

Mrs. Reid introduced from the audience two Nobel Prize winners, Dr. Joliot Curie, who was in New York on his way to the atom bomb test in Bikini, and Dr. Otto Loewi. Then myself. After amenities, I staked out some ground rules for the trip:

I have no wish to search for sweetness and light, for good food and well-being, of which I hear there is pitifully little abroad. I have no wish to deny the painfully disagreeable aspects of the state of almost every nation. I will not go out of my way to avoid areas of disturbance any more than I will seek them out, but it seems to me that the day-to-day foment of our world is being wonderfully well documented and reported by our colleagues of press and radio, and I would not be so rash as to attempt to "case" a country after an exhaustive study of three days.

Together with Mr. Bland and the recording equipment, which CBS has furnished us, I intend to concentrate on evidence of repair and mending, to listen for sounds of the construction of better things and better times, to watch for indications of oneness everywhere.

For the other side of it, for the evidences of deteriorating relationships, for the sound of despair and cynicism, of defeatism and general gloom, one need not stir from his living room. Nothing can be darker in the world outside us than the dispatches of darkness, which we read here at home. Surely nobody needs the services of another pallbearer. It is no longer unique to view with despondent suspicion an ally. What is unique is to view an ally with respect and trust and tolerance, with perhaps the slightest remembrance and appreciation of the common struggle so few months behind us.

I made a discovery recently in as mild and unexpected a source as a dictionary of one of the things that seem to be symptomatic of our troubles. Webster defines the word "diplomacy" as "The artful management of securing advantages without arousing hostility." Now, the editors offer this with a straight face, apparently unaware that in most modern history, diplomacy has consisted of the artful management of arousing hostility without securing advantages. But perhaps with the reshuffling of terms corollary to the establishment of a single world, Webster can be influenced to rewrite their definition to read, "The artful management of securing amity, which is of the highest mutual advantage."

The One World Award is, in a sense, a mechanism of a hope. My relationship to it is that of a small, moving part in the machine. The Awards Committee, CBS, I, and, I hope, you are pulling for good results. But in the event of failure, either of the machine or of this particular moving part, the basic principle of One World, the quest for means to implement and establish it, must never be abandoned, neither in our time nor in the time, if it takes that long, of a distant generation of our children.

Much publicity had attached to the flight before it was even off the ground, so it was only natural, I suppose, that the departure had to be public too. Ferrand, CBS programing VP Davidson Taylor, George Field, Executive Director of Freedom House, Reinhold Schairer, of the World Education Service Council, six children representing the World Friendship Council, Pan-American Airways personnel, my family, and a few friends, all came out to LaGuardia—along with Harry Kramer of CBS, and the technical men necessary to do a 15-minute broadcast from the plane gate.

My mother cried a little and I tried to be bluff and hearty and confident. What I did not know at the time, for she had kept it from me, was that she was going to be operated upon for cancer during my absence from the country. She thought she was saying goodbye to me forever—an apprehension happily not borne out, since the operation was successful. [Mrs. Corwin lived for another 16 years.]

At the plane there were photographers and some posing. At last we boarded a great Constellation named CLIPPER 60, and sat behind Juan Trippe, president of Pan-American, who was aboard because the flight was inaugurating commercial service between New York and Calcutta. We took off at 11:20. Lee and I lost very little time getting forward to the Navigation Station, and within half an hour we were recording some of my observations.

Banks of the Channel
England and France

*the experience was thrilling in
the full sense of the word*

Not long before landing at our first stop in Gander, Newfound-land, a ruddy faced, grey-haired man stopped to watch while Lee and I were taking pictures and he made some comments about photography. He introduced himself: Vladimir Hurban, Czech ambassador to the United States, on his way to Prague. He said he knew something of my work, having heard my program about Czechoslovakia, "The Long Name None Could Spell." "How did you come up so fast?" he asked. "Only in America," I said.

We had a fine chat about the hanging of Nazi Karl Hermann Frank by the Czechs, which I had seen recently in the newsreels. "I urged American newsreel companies to release the pictures," Hurban said. "They resisted because of the grimness of the subject, but some of them finally agreed. And now I wonder whether it was the right thing to have done."

I said I thought it very important to release such reels, inasmuch as the world so soon forgets the Nazi brutality and should be reminded. We talked also of the movement to build a stone monument at Lidice, which I declined to join some time ago when asked to serve on an American committee, because I felt the memorial should be a living one. He said that he, and in fact the Czechs themselves, agreed.

London was changed since I had seen it last, and the difference was all to the good. There were no barrage balloons overhead, no signs pointing to air raid shelters, no fresh bomb ruins. It was early on a Sunday morning, and, as we drove in from the airport, the city was still sleeping and the streets bare. Hyde Park was quiet as a country dell.

Martha Gellhorn [then Mrs. Ernest Hemingway] shared a taxi with Bland and me as we rode in from the airport. She was fresh and bright after twelve hours in the air, and chatted buoyantly. Bland was glazed with fatigue, and in retirement. I, bearded, fagged, bleary, mumbled a few times to show I was awake, and hated her for being so resilient.

The morning was warm and fair—one of the few legitimately summery days in any English year. By night it was raining, and even indoors it was chilly. I found people were eating the same dull food in the same cold rooms, as during the darkest days of 1942. It was now 13 months since the end of the war in Europe, but this country which had withstood the Nazis alone for a year, was still pinched.

The morning after we arrived, the government announced that the milk ration would be cut, the soap ration reduced by one seventh, and that rationing of bread would end soon. I asked a housewife about conditions—a middle class housewife named Mrs. Hill, and she was almost gay in her seeming unconcern. She said she was getting one egg every two months, and two pints of milk per week. I asked her about the availability and variety of other foods, and how the fare compared to the days of the war:

> **Mrs. Hill:** Well, I think it's a little better now. For instance, last week, I got two pounds of strawberries, but that's because I have dealt with the same man for eight years. He knows me very well. He goes in the back of the shop and comes out with his finger up to his mouth, saying, "Shush," and he puts something in the bottom of my bag and I can't ask what it is.

NC: Did you ask what the price was?

Mrs. Hill: Oh heavens no! I wouldn't dare to.

NC: But what was the price?

Mrs. Hill: I don't know.

NC: You will be billed at the end of the month?

Mrs. Hill: I shall be billed at the end of the month, and I shall put up my hands in horror and ask for another box.

NC: How long has it been since you've had a meal at home which was really filling, so that you felt you might have to stagger away from the table?

Mrs. Hill: Christmas.

NC: Once a year then?

Mrs. Hill: Well, once a year, yes; but then, I wangled that. You see, I knew somebody in the country who knew a farmer who sent a goose, and we ate it in one day. Three of us—a 20-pound goose.

NC: In any season other than Christmas would that be rash and headstrong?

Mrs. Hill: Oh it certainly would.

Mrs. Hill had enough money to be prudent and not ask the price of strawberries. But for those less well off in England (as everywhere else, including the United States) there was never the 20-pound goose, not even on Christmas. Beginning in London clear around the world to Los Angeles, I was to find very few cities where food for the majority of people was ample and varied and cheap. Black markets for those who could pay, but for low incomes or none, it was the old routine, ranging from not-quite-enough-to-eat, to sheer starvation.

But other things besides food were on the minds of the English people and their government at this moment, and I set out to learn what a few of them were. I made an appointment to record the Prime Minister, Clement Attlee, at 10 Downing Street. He received me in the Cabinet Room where so many decisions fateful to the world had been made in recent history. He was alone except for his secretary, Francis Williams. Attlee wore a cardigan sweater, and puffed a pipe with an expression of ease and absorption. Francis Williams made clear to me that the Prime Minister had never been recorded in this manner; that, like the President of the United States, he always spoke, for radio purposes, over several networks, never to an individual one. But in deference to the auspices of the One World Award, an exception was being made.

That summer, international tension was high; against this background, I asked Attlee whether he felt there were any chances that Willkie's ideas could make headway:

> **Attlee:** Well, I don't think we ought to get despondent too early or too easily because of the international difficulties and the suspicions and opposing interests. After all, we're trying to clean up after the greatest war in history and you can't expect all the problems of that war, and a good many left over from the first World War, to disappear overnight. The trouble is, of course, all the differences make for dramatic news.
>
> **NC:** Have you any ideas about what might be termed the techniques of peace?
>
> **Attlee:** One important thing is, first of all, to realize that there's something quite different in "Peace" from "No More War." If you continually think of the prevention of war, you don't get very far. You've got to think of positive peace.
>
> And that really depends on a greater understanding, not just between governments but between peoples, not just about policies, but about ways of life. That enterprise is quite as exciting and quite as adventurous as anything you ever had in war.

In my next interview, this principle got a concurring opinion. I looked up J. B. Priestley, who had written trenchantly on social and political subjects throughout the war. Only a few days before, he had returned from a trip to the Scandinavia and the Soviet

Union. He came to Claridge's, where Bland and I were installed, and talked to our microphone as to an old friend:

Priestley: There is a great danger now, I think, of what psychologists call "projecting the contents of the subconscious onto the outside world." In other words, instead of trying to understand other people, you project the contents of the unconscious that you don't like—the evil bit of yourself—onto these other people as if they were a blank wall and you were throwing a lantern slide on. And there's a great deal of that happening. I think one reason why the victorious Allies began drawing away from each other the minute their common enemies were defeated, was that they were still busy continuing in the same psychological mood, and finding, inventing enemies, almost. You see the drift of my remarks?

NC: I do. What would you recommend as a means of correcting this?

Priestley: People must have access to information about other countries. They must see the cultural products of other countries, and if possible, they must be able to move about the world freely, as soon as transport is available. Because democracy is based on information, on trying to get the facts somehow. And you'll find that the greatest enemies of any progressive world organization are the people who don't know . . . who really live in fantastic worlds of their own, who don't know Britain, who don't know Russia, don't know China or India or anywhere else. I don't say the traveled man is always the wise man, but I do say you're more likely, if you've been to these places, to know that they're real people there, and not monsters.

The next man interviewed, Minister of State Philip Noel-Baker, went beyond that, to say that not only must information be free, but uncolored; that it must not be distorted to fit a publisher's or broadcaster's personal political prejudice, or angled in the interests of sensationalism and circulation. Our meeting took place in the foreign office, an old building just across the way from the

Prime Minister's office. Portraits of antiquity and dignity, none of whose subjects I recognized, looked sternly down:

> **Noel-Baker:** I admire and believe in the work Wendell Willkie did. I doubt that since he wrote his book, I've made a single important speech in which, directly or indirectly, I have not referred to Willkie and "One World" . . . everything we are trying to do in the United Nations, if it is to succeed, must be founded on that fundamental concept.
>
> But unless behind the United Nations we have a really strong and instructed public opinion, the thing will fail. I confess that I think most publicity magnates are falling into a very grave error when they believe as they do believe now, that only quarrels and disputes are news. In our Economic and Social Council work in New York last week, we had many discussions in which every single speech made, whether it was by the United States delegate, or by the United Kingdom delegate or by the Soviet delegate or the Yugoslavian, was in fact a constructive speech intended to help towards a long term result; and yet nearly all the newspapers came out day by day, if they mentioned a thing at all, with a heading "Anglo-Soviet Clash." There was indeed a point on which we were not in agreement with the Soviet Union, but taking the discussion as a whole, it was an utter misrepresentation of the facts.
>
> I suppose *magna est veritas*, and in the end it will prevail—but what I do mind is the utter stupidity of the publicity magnates in thinking that the people want to go on reading about the clashes after eight years of appeasement and six years of total war.

Back at Claridge's, Bland and I were hosts at tea to Lord and Lady Robert Van Sittart. Lord Van Sittart had been in the diplomatic service for 44 of his 65 years, was first Baron of Denhain, a Conservative member of parliament, and the author of half a dozen books, including *People Like Ourselves*. He struck me as having the gentility and strong cast of mind that, so often among

British aristocracy, are not accidents of fortune or birth, but are achieved. We talked long of Germany and the special problems she presented, and then issues of censorship:

Van Sittart: People talk a great deal about an iron curtain, but peacetime censorship exists in many parts of the world. In the United States, there is supposed to be complete freedom from censorship, yet a dispatch coming from a correspondent in Eastern Europe, when sent to a newspaper that holds an extreme point of view, will not always be printed as sent. They will allow nothing of a contrary point of view to be printed.

NC: Then you are saying that censorship, whether it comes from an outside government or an inside publisher, all adds up to the same thing?

Van Sittart: Yes, on the whole, you in the United States suffer from it rather more than we do here. There are more papers in the United States than here with a definite ax to grind, and they mean to grind it at any price, and so they not only end but begin by adopting the attitude which I've just described. That is most unfortunate, because these newspapers have a very large circulation. They're got a circulation of between 12 and 15 million, or something of that sort. It's unhappy that anything in the nature of censorship should be imposed for the purposes of politics, don't you think so?

Totalitarian states don't allow their publics to hear anything that doesn't suit their mood of the moment or their ulterior motives. In the democratic countries there's far too great a tendency to allow encroachment upon foreign affairs, by domestic affairs. That accounts for the phenomenon that some newspapers only print what happens to suit their particular party outlook. The readers only hear what happens to suit the management of the newspaper. That, on a much smaller scale, is the same thing that is practiced by totalitarian governments. It makes really rather a vicious circle. I believe both these things have got to be broken.

After the meeting with Lord Van Sittart, our recorder went haywire. We found out about it in the course of ruining an interview with Sir Alexander Fleming, the discoverer of penicillin, whom we met in his laboratory in the inoculation division at drab St. Mary's Hospital in Paddington. It was an unsatisfactory meeting in more respects than mechanical, since Sir Alexander seemed shy of the microphone, by nature laconic, and, though hospitable, somewhat ill at ease. He looked out from behind spectacles whose lenses seemed to have no curvature whatever, just flat pieces of glass, and they kept catching the light in a series of disconcerting flashes. I thought to maneuver him toward another position, but it was awkward to suggest, so I just kept talking as though to an intermittent beacon. He had almost a pugilist's nose, and a brogue that was light for a born Scotsman. His bow tie gave him a youthful look against his white hair. On the wall behind him was a set of reproductions of Pioneers of Painting by the American Dean Cornwall, and a silver plaque presented to him by the Variety Club during a recent visit he made to the States.

Sir Alexander told me the laboratory in which we were meeting was founded by the man who introduced anti-typhoid serum, and was chiefly a vaccine laboratory. "Antibiotic research here is merely an incident . . . it was spare-time research. We were not equipped with perfect antibiotic materials, so we could not pursue the thing to the final end."

I asked him whether broad governmental use of drugs such as penicillin, might someday rid the world completely of social diseases:

> **Fleming:** You've got to get the patient to come to treatment. If the patient does not come for his treatment you can't treat him. The government may force him to come for treatment. Is that unwarrantable interference with the freedom of the subject?

That set us off on twenty minutes of discussion, all of which was lost to the record because of a flaw in the machine. At the end of the recording, Sir Alexander sighed and said, "It wasn't as bad as I thought it was going to be."

Neither Bland nor all the king's technicians of the BBC were able to clear up the obliterating hum in our machine. As a result, my later interviews in London with factory workers, a bus driver, a student, a doctor, a farmer, went without the modest immortality proposed by magnetic wire.

I left London with the same impression of a strong and confident British people that I had carried away when I was last among them during a bleak period of the war. We drove to Northolt and boarded a plane for Paris. It took off into a stormy sky and flew at a low level over the poetic country of Kent and Sussex. We sat on cushioned seats, riding through skies that had been the greatest aerial battlefield in history. This way had come the Luftwaffe, and gone back broken; this way had come the night raiders and the buzz-bombs and the V-rockets; this way had gone the Stirlings and Lancasters, the Liberators and the B-17's.

We crossed the coast at Bexhill and headed for France. The weather over the channel was clear, and the water sparkled with facets of reflected sunlight, a sheet of green marble veined with white. I looked out of the window at the bright strait and found myself thinking of Paddy Finucane, who died down there one afternoon.

We landed on steel matting, at Le Bourget, and drove in to the city through Pissaro countryside and Utrillo streets. My stay in France was only a week, but that was long enough to see a cabinet fall, meet a hundred assorted Frenchmen, and be reminded of how beautiful Paris is. It is one of the few cities in the world that lives up to the paintings done of it. You have only to walk down its avenues and side streets and along the Seine to understand why Paris is not to be compared to any other city. You sit on a bench in the Tuileries and understand why writers and painters and composers and peace conferences have always been attracted to it.

Paris was still beautiful in 1946, but there was none of the old gaiety. The war, while it left the city intact, did things to its people. Too many Frenchmen died in the torture chambers of the Gestapo, too many went hungry, too many had experience with collaborators, too many shivered in the cold.

On the day we got there, the city was turbulent. There was a demonstration by 200,000 Communists in protest over a recent attack on their headquarters. It was nonetheless peaceful, and there was more of a holiday mood than grimness. One of the most forceful impressions of France at that hour, was the taking-for-granted of Communists as fixtures in the political scene.

The biggest advertising in the city looked down on the Opera House from across the Place de L'Opera—a sign advertising the newspaper *Humanite*, and bearing the emblem of the hammer and sickle. The Communists had just made gains in recent elections, and were then the second strongest party in France. The coalition cabinet of Georges Bidault was even then forming. The first man I Interviewed was Maurice Schumann, official spokesman for Bidault's party—the Movement Republican Francaise. Schumann, who was very close to De Gaulle during the war, was especially tough on the subject of Germany:

> **Schumann:** I think it suicidal for both East and West to build Germany up in their respective spheres. For, then, Germany will unite, and German union within is the inverse of unity without. I believe, we should at once share the secret of the atom bomb with Russia, who has suffered hurt pride in her diplomatic setbacks up to now. I feel leadership in world affairs rests with the United States, as a country with no territorial or imperialist ambitions.

I interviewed Schumann in his small flat on Avenue Lyatey, and during our conversation his infant son was crying in the next room. Had our recorder not been still out of action—I might have preserved the son's cries over the father's opinions. Bland, after trying to get the horror box fixed by French technicians, in desperation flew with the machine to Frankfurt in the hope that American army engineers could diagnose the trouble.

Even in introspective France, one could rely on scientists to think internationally. Frederic Joliot-Curie, descendant of Eve Curie and himself a Nobel Prize winner in chemistry, was no exception. This was the year when scientists for the first time were coming out of the laboratory to take more active roles as citizens. After recalling his presence at the send-off luncheon in the Waldorf-Astoria, Joliot-Curie got quickly to the meat:

> **Joliot-Curie:** It cannot be denied that the conscience of the scientific world is undergoing a crisis, and that the collective sense of social responsibility is gathering strength.
>
> **NC:** Does today's scientist think of himself as a citizen of the world? And if he does, should he have a troubled conscience?
>
> **Joliot-Curie:** You must first consider the place of the scientist in the national community, whose labor creates the material condition of his existence and work. Scientists and technicians do not and cannot belong to a detached state. As citizens and members of the great community of creators and workers, they must be concerned with the use society makes of their discoveries, and with practical ways of directing this use towards peace and the well-being of mankind.

Almost everybody I met in Paris had a story to tell that sounded more like an exciting novel. A young Zionist, Sylvan, who said, "I fought with the Yugoslav partisans; if there are any better fighters in the world, I haven't met them"; Marie, a Polish girl who literally escaped from the Germans on her way to a gas chamber; Paul Derme, who was devoting his life to the internationalization of radio; Robert Carne, film director, who was disturbed because "The French public looks down on films as a poor relative among the arts"; Andre Siegfried of the French Academy: "I am quite set in my belief that art and politics do not mix"; Paul Nelson, American architect and special consultant to the French Ministry of Reconstruction:

> **Nelson:** As long as there remains the vestiges of fascism any place, the people of France, and of America, and of the world, are in danger. I don't think that Bikini represented a great day for American influence. The great day will be when the experiment will be centered on the utilization of atomic energy for the peaceful benefit of mankind.

Then there was blonde Natya, a pianist, whose father had died
of malnutrition and cold, whose brother had been killed fighting
Nazis on the day before Paris was liberated, who herself had fired
shots in the same battle. Paris was full of people like that. They all
wanted peace, and they were shaking fists at nobody.

The symbol of war in France, as in other occupied countries,
had been the resistance. The fighters of the underground were
above ground now, sharing the toils of peace and reconstruction. The most eloquent voice of the resistance was that of Louis
Aragon, about whom the *Saturday Review of Literature* had recently
written: "It seems clear today that Louis Aragon is the greatest
poet of the war." Aragon had served with an armored division,
was captured by the Nazis, broke out of prison, and fought on
with the Maquis. For his exploits he received the highest French
Military decoration.

> **Aragon:** I remember somewhere near Chateau Thiery—it was in
> 1918—the coming of American men. We were leaving the
> lines in the middle of the night with all the carefulness of
> old and wise warriors, silently, when we heard a huge noise
> of men, horses, trucks, songs, cries, jokes; and in the dark we
> saw the lighting of matches, pipes. American soldiers took
> our place, and the next day we saw them—a lot of them—
> wounded, killed, taken back by the wonderful American
> cars we admired so much.
>
> It takes ages, you know, to be taught to be silent and not
> to light one's pipe when going up to the lines. The American
> men were new to the war. They fought as one plays baseball.
> They were marvelous, and they helped to the victory, as one
> can tell now. But the price, the terrible prices!
>
> Well, the experience of one generation is never passed
> to another. It took very long till the American people could
> be persuaded [their] interest was to fight on our side in
> Europe. I am quite sure it took a long time for the boys
> to realize what war really was. They fought magnificently.
> I know.

This time also, we were full of admiration for Americans when we saw them all over France. But, don't you understand, it all could have been avoided. War could have been avoided, and the coming of your boys into the heart of death, and the price you paid once more. And why had it not been avoided? Why had all that to be lived all over once more? Because you—because we—lacked memory. Because we didn't remember what we had been told. And this will be again and again the same thing, if we again and again don't teach ourselves not to forget.

It has been endlessly spoken about "Wilson's mistake." This time people say in America, "We ought to participate in European affairs." But it's not just a question of participation. The matter of memory must be understood not only by American leaders, but by all the American people; and one must know also what is to be remembered.

What is America for a Frenchman? The country where it was said, "Government of the people, by the people and for the people." This cannot be a slogan for Americans only. We love Lincoln's America. It is always Lincoln's America that we cheer and greet. When American boys come to France against a common enemy, it is Lincoln's America— the generous democratic America we love—which twice in thirty years gave us its strong helpful hand in our fight against the Germans of Wilhelm II and the SS of Hitler. It is the high principles of Lincoln's America which must be first remembered, in order to achieve a world without wars.

And what we want, we Frenchmen, is first that our American friends will never listen to those of our countrymen who would have armed Lincoln's murderer, if they had been Americans themselves and had lived in his time. There have been too many of that type of Frenchman heard in America during the years we were here fighting our lonely difficult fight. Lincoln's America must also remember something else . . . that modern war is not only fought on the lines against men in uniforms, against foreigners.

The man who killed Lincoln is also the enemy. Lincoln's America must know that Germans do not historically stay on their soil—that they invade our country periodically for devious purposes; and it is in them to *kill* "government of the people of France, by the people of France and for the people of France."

We want to live in peace. We want all nations of Europe and the world to live in peace with us. That is why we tell you, our American friends, you must not forget France.

In the name of humanity there are people who speak of forgetting Nazi crimes because Germany must live; but humanity should not forget the men and women who were killed and tortured by Hitler's Germany. I speak for memory—I speak for active memory against war. For the sake of American boys, we do not want to meet every 25 years on French soil. Active memory in France and in America, conscious memory of inside and outside enemies.

In the absence of our portable equipment, Aragon had been recorded on an acetate disc. Bland came back from Frankfurt with the wire recorder still useless. American and German specialists had not been able to figure it out. It was impossible then to buy another such machine in Europe. We had to drag the damn thing along, with its heavy spools of wire, to Scandinavia. We packed and took off for Copenhagen.

Clouds obscured the face of France, Belgium and Holland, but lifted over the coast of Germany. We caught glimpses of the North Sea and the outlying Danish islands, with their rich green fields, red-roofed farmhouses, and herds at pasture. Having flown over the territory of five countries in four hours, we landed on Copenhagen's Kastrup airfield, which the Nazis had seized without warning on an infamous day in May, six years ago.

3

Peace in the North
Denmark, Norway, Sweden

The light outside had the quality of dawn

Denmark was never intended to be a working stop, not because it had no attractions for our log, but because flying-schedule complications had all but dropped it from the itinerary. But Ferrand had forgotten this, and sent advance notice of our arrival to the Danish Ministry of Information. At Kastrup we were surprised to be met by reporters, photographers, a man from the American Legation, another from the Danish Foreign Office, and the press chief of the Danish State Radio, Paul Berg.

When I told Berg we were only staying overnight, he was astonished. I realized I was treading on eggshells, for no person, let alone a ministry, likes to be considered incidental. Hastily I elaborated on our flying complications, explained that we had to be in Oslo the following night in order to make long reserved connections for eastern Europe, and said I was eager to meet as many representative Danes as could be crowded into the time available.

Berg had handled tougher situations than this. He started making telephone calls from the airport, while I talked to reporters. Then he came to the Hotel Angleterre, installed himself in my room, and kept on the telephone until past midnight, lining up interviews for the next day, and arranging for recording facilities to be set up

29

in the Parliament building. He left with instructions to meet him next morning at the radio headquarters, Statsradiofonibyningen. In the morning I asked a taxi driver to take us to Statsradiofonibyningen. So crisply and cleanly did I enunciate this name that he delivered us to the railroad station. When we finally reached it, I understood why Berg was so anxious for us to see Radio House before starting the day's work. It was then, and still may be, the finest radio installation in the world.

The exterior was simple and rather primly administrative, except for a pleasantly broad, shallow dome, which crowned a concert studio of 2,100 seats. The dome, with its subtle contour, saved the external aspect from too great a severity. Within, all was light and magic: free, naked staircases of teakwood; walls and panels of worked beach wood, birch and teak; lavish use of parquet floors, undulating ceilings, studio roof gardens, trees and shrubs enchantingly related to interior corridors and passages; lighting fixtures as only the Danes make them; a concert hall of regal dignity and flowing lines, with a mighty pipe organ (no Hammond electric in *this* studio) rising behind the orchestra platform. It was not one building, really, but an interlocking complex: a multi-storied office section of two wings, a Champs Elysee of studios (music on the right, drama on the left); a manager's residence, and four flats for employees.

Copenhagen was suffering from an acute housing shortage, but seemed in good physical shape. There was rationing of some commodities, although nothing severe. Denmark showed the least damage of any of the occupied countries, a distinction none would begrudge her. But whatever she had gone through was bad enough. Danes with whom I talked filled me in: It was another catalogue of Nazi atrocities, so much like those elsewhere in Europe. But there was this difference to the story: no occupied people showed more open contempt, or went about their acts of resistance and sabotage with such panache.

The Nazis, when they first took over, went to the length, for propaganda purposes, of allowing a free election. Had the populace buckled or worried about reprisals, they might have voted for local Nazi candidates, but the Danish Nazis polled less than 2 percent of the vote. The protection by Denmark of its Jews was also unlike anything in any other country under the Nazi yoke. The Gestapo made plans to round up all Jews in the country on the night of October 1–2, 1943. But thanks to the underground and the support of the entire Danish population, only 472 were caught; nearly 9,000 were safely spirited across Ore Sound to Sweden, a triumph of logistics, secrecy and humanity.

To an anteroom of the Parliament, which was in full session, Berg led a series of government officials to be interviewed. They included Finance Minister Torkil Kristensen, Minister for Special Affairs Per Federspiel, former Foreign Minister Christmas Moller, and the incumbent foreign minister, Gustav Rasmussen, a tall, gaunt man who could have doubled for Serge Rachmaninoff. Also on the roster, so that we would not be top heavy with brass, were a farmer, a mechanic, a schoolboy, a writer named Hans Seedorf. All spoke English. Of the interviews, Rasmussen's was the most helpful on the theme of the journey. In part:

NC: Do you think we are headed for another war?

Rasmussen: No, I don't, I don't see any reason why a new war should separate us in our time, and I don't believe it will.

NC: What do you consider the principal sources of friction?

Rasmussen: Distrust combined with fear. Mutual suspicion.

NC: What can be done to allay suspicion?

Rasmussen: Frankness would be a great help. In general, to be less afraid of each other, and of each other's opinion.

NC: Don't you think a civilization ingenious enough to produce radio, the airplane and the atom bomb, might also be ingenious enough to conduct international relations on a calm and logical basis?

Rasmussen: Yes, I certainly do; but on the other hand, don't forget that political relations between states are sometimes more complicated than one would think on the face of it- even more difficult to handle than mechanical inventions.

I asked whether Denmark, situated as she was between East
and West, might be tempted to join any power bloc. He said he
wanted to answer that question more thoughtfully than might be
expressed in the give-and-take of our discussion, and volunteered
to cable a statement to me the following day, to reach me in Sweden. He kept his word. The message, arriving on a telegram form,
was all in lower case:

> of natural resources denmark has only her soil. denmark pos-
> sesses neither coal nor metals and has no large forests such as
> norway sweden and finland. neither has she great rivers and
> waterfalls to turn into sources of power. so evidently denmark
> cannot isolate herself economically and has no wish to do so.
> it is of vital interest to us to live in a peaceful world in which we
> can sail the seven seas and trade with other nations. denmark
> trusts she can retain her traditional democratic method of work-
> ing out her internal problems and will carry on her foreign
> policy within the framework of the united nations. denmark is
> not prepared to participate in any combination of powers that
> might be regarded as a potential threat by other nations
>
> gustav rasmussen

But that was in Sweden, and is ahead of the schedule. It was
not yet noon of our only day in Copenhagen, and all the interviewing had been done. Berg announced it was time for lunch, and we
started off with him. Instead of heading directly for a restaurant,
he pulled up at the magnificently bizarre Town Hall, a stalwart
blend of granite, limestone, rust-red brick and terra cotta, with
cross-breedings of Danish and Italian architecture. Its five tiers of
windows, looking out on the Raadhuspladsen, were wildly different from each other: two huge oriels stood like sentinels half way
up the building, equidistant from a noble arched entrance at the
center. Battlements along the roof would have been at home on a
medieval tower. Yet it all came together, strangely, with the dignity
and charm characteristic of the older city. An architect was quoted
as saying of the Raadhus, "It was worth doing once, but I hope
nobody but a Dane tries it again—It would be a mess."

We felt it was thoughtful of Berg to stop on the way to lunch, to show us the inside of Town Hall. He told us, as we entered, that it held six hundred rooms, and then proceeded to take us into several of them. One, especially grandiose, was a municipal dining room, where a long table was heaped with food. Twenty men were ranged on both sides of the table, waiting for us. Mayor (Borgmester) Alfred Binslev, in the name of the city, was feting two overnight visitors.

The party consisted of members of the City Council, three members of Parliament, two cabinet ministers, and Berg. There were formal toasts, with the schnapps glass held at a ritualistically prescribed level, raised, extended, returned to the third button of the vest or thereabouts, and then swigged in turn with each member of the table. I was unschooled in these things, and drank easily, as one would in the Barberry Room. Worse yet, I rose and replied immediately to the Mayor's address of welcome. Nobody told me about those things. I should have waited until the next-to-last course. I found that out later, in Sweden, in time to avoid similar faux pas in the company of royalty. The Danes were of course too polite to correct me, and Bland knew from as close to nothing as I.

Altogether, I was treated in Denmark as though I were a defeated presidential candidate; let nobody say that only Italians, of peoples on the Continent, are conspicuously warm. So are the Danes, a hearty, brave and generous people. At that moment in their history, having come through a costly and bloody occupation, and having still to support 210,000 German civilian evacuees who had been dumped in Denmark when the Allied armies closed in on Berlin (at a cost to Denmark of twice its budget for education), the Danes nevertheless found the will and wherewithal to contribute 143,000,000 krone to a Norwegian relief fund, 17,000,000 worth of food parcels to a hungry Netherlands, 2,000,000 for relief work in France, 6,000,000 for Finnish children, and similar contributions to Belgium, Czechoslovakia, Poland, Austria and Hungary.

We left Copenhagen in bright sunshine at 9 p.m. and flew due north, along the arms of the North Sea known by the crunching names of Kattegat and Skagerrak. The northern sun blazed red in the sky and our Danish DC3 pointed its nose straight toward it. At 10:15 p.m. Norwegian time, the sun was still bright, and although it sank below the horizon a half hour later, we could easily make out, in the lingering twilight, the excitingly beautiful and complex Christiania Fjord, at the apex of which sits Oslo.

Nobody met us at Fornebu airport. It was the reverse of the reception at Kastrup. Our reservations had gone amiss, or been pigeonholed; Ferrand's advance notice, including a shortwave broadcast to Norway by its Ambassador Morganstierne in Washington, to the effect that we were coming, had apparently missed somehow. The airport personnel were thinned out by this hour, being close to midnight, and those who remained spoke no English. Bland and I tried to find out, using pay phones, where and whether we had lodgings and a place to stow our 200-pound casket of useless equipment. But no operator spoke English. Not even the telephone dial was familiar. Its numbers progressed in reverse order to American phones, which is to say, counter-clockwise from 10 to 0.

Bland discovered in his little black address book the telephone number of Einar Haugen, United States Information Service, and took the desperate measure of awakening him. Haugen sleepily remembered word having come through the American Embassy about our impending arrival, but was under the impression it was for later in the week. He told us to go to a billet where people attached to the Embassy were lodged.

We reached Camilla Colletts Vie 15, after midnight. The northern sky was light, as though dawn were breaking, and I could not overcome the sensation of having been up all night. Though I was not tired, the intimation of approaching day teased me into the belief that I *should* be. Since it was light enough to read by, brighter than the light of a full moon, Bland thought to improve the moment by taking photographs that he could show back home. But the midnight sun is not a toy of amateur photographers: nothing came out.

As Paul Berg had been our host in Copenhagen, Karl Gastren Lyche, Director of the Norwegian State Radio, was in Oslo. For services to the underground, the Nazis had clapped him into a concentration camp, but until then he had been kept at his radio post. One day when Vidkun Quisling, the infamous traitor who helped Germany prepare for the conquest of Norway, was scheduled to broadcast, Lyche refused to cooperate. But to Lyche's surprise, he was not punished by the Germans. "They rather despised Quisling themselves," he explained.

What a perfect name for a traitor is Quisling. It sounds close to weasling, and the "-ling" suffix in English connotes contempt, as in "hireling." It is not every knave who gives his name irrevocably to the language, so integrated as to be found in the main vocabulary. When a name appears in lower case, then it has truly taken hold, whether the nominating essence be honorable or notorious, Not even Philippic and Caesarian can claim lower case initial letters, although alexandrine has it both ways.

Before presenting me to recordable Norwegians, Mr. Lyche introduced me to whale meat at a restaurant on Hegdehaugsveien off Pilestredet, a mouthful by itself. I expected a fishy taste, and was wrong. It was like pot roast. But I am glad whale steak is not a staple of universal diet. The whale has a hard enough time staying ahead of extinction, without being hunted for the chef. He is one of my favorite mammals, one of the few superb relics of an age of amplitude, like the redwood tree and the rhinoceros.

Like Copenhagen and Paris, Oslo had not been damaged much. The city is small, arid although not resplendent, its natural situation gives it a distinction few cities inherit. Oslo was substantial, modern in character, and also crowded when we were there; rationing of most commodities was severe. Fuel was low; we shaved with cold water.

The people of the city were still relaxing from the strain of the war; it had not worn off yet. They had had five years of occupation; their resistance had been as tough as that of the Danes. They had given the Nazis a workout, including the sinking of a German cruiser in Oslofjord within hours of the attack on April 9, 1940.

Haakon Lie, secretary of Norway's Labor Party, told me that the industrial population suffered tremendously during the war, and that "the psychological pressure was much greater than any American can imagine." I asked him whether Norwegians were interested in international affairs or whether they, like the French, were more absorbed by internal problems. He answered: "We're a very small nation, but we are more interested in the outside world than any other nation I know."

One night I met a group of underground men that included Sigurd Evensmo, sole survivor of a band of 18 Norwegians who were caught off the west coast of Norway, trying to escape to England. An informer, one of their party, had turned them into the Gestapo—for 700 crowns—an average of about ten dollars per head. All but Evensmo were executed; he escaped death by the lucky accident of having been suspected of *two* crimes against the Nazis. With typical Nazi thoroughness whenever going through motions of judicial process, they decided to hold Evensmo for investigation of the second, equally capital, crime. The delay gave him a chance to break prison. I asked Evensmo, a journalist and novelist, why the Nazis so deeply hated the intellectuals.

Evensmo: I suppose because they knew they could expect the hardest resistance from them as good patriots, and also because the Nazis had—what do you call it . . .

Lyche: Crushed all rights.

Evensmo: Yes—and an intellectual is the first to recognize when rights have been crushed. Not all intellectuals. But in this country, most.

Lyche: Back in 1940, we were told many times, "The Germans are going to win the war, so you might as well arrange yourselves with them." My personal reply to that was, well, if the Germans win there will be no use living, so why not rather commit myself and die resisting them. To the same extent, the same situation exists today. If we can't bring the feeling of One World and hope to all nations, if we can't make them understand the necessity of mutual trust, there will be no use living 30 years from now. So even though I'm a bit pessimistic by nature, I'm an optimist by deliberation.

Another of the group was Dr. H.O. Christophersen, a doctor of philosophy, who held a vital and dangerous liaison post in the resistance movement.

During the occupation we were faced with a very strong power, a physical power, and nobody in his senses would beforehand have thought we had a ghost of a chance against that power. But in point of fact, we very soon felt that we had a good chance, indeed very soon we thought we were *superior.* That gave us a new knowledge, you might say, of that most important of all political concepts of what is power. I think that if, for instance, you could make some of your prominent American political scientists study, from a scientific point of view, our experiences during the war in this particular respect, it would be of service, for it might make people understand that *mind, spirit, will, morality* have a very good chance against physical power, even when prospects look very bad.

The foreign minister of Norway was Halyard Lange. Statesmanship was in his family—his father had been prominent in the League of Nations. Young, handsome enough to play Bill Holden roles, soft-spoken, he came with a prepared script but put it aside to answer my questions:

NC: Do you feel there has been irreparable deterioration of international relations since the end of the war? Enough to justify despair or cynicism?

Lange: It has been disappointing to see wartime cooperation and solidarity unable to live down a certain mutual distrust. But there are deep historic reasons for that; and as long as one can see reasons, one need not despair. To my mind, even though we may have disastrous setbacks from time to time, we must never give up faith in the possibility of reaching international understanding. Old habits and traditions cannot be changed in a few months, even in a few years—and this is a new world, transforming itself before our eyes. We shall certainly need all the optimism we can manage.

NC: Are you optimistic yourself?

Lange: Yes. Norway during the war was considered hopelessly, foolishly optimistic by the Germans. Optimism is a very positive element.

NC: Certainly psychological factors have been powerful in all wars. What you said about having less to fear if we know the reasons for distrust, is, I am sure, close to the core of psychoanalysis as practiced on the individual. This almost suggests a parallel between the insecurity fears of the individual, and those of the state.

Lange: You must always be careful in drawing parallels between individual and corporate phenomena, but I agree that if we can get to the roots of problems and understand them, we have made a great step toward resolving the difficulty.

NC: Has Norway's attitude toward the United States changed appreciably since the war?

Lange: It has not changed, except perhaps that the temperature of our feelings may have become even higher than before. Way back in 1814, our Constitution was strongly influenced by your Declaration of Independence. We have always trusted in America taking the lead, when need be, in the fight for the rights of free men. Our hopes have not been disappointed.

NC: Do you feel that the phrase "all men are created equal" has added force and meaning today?

Lange: Yes. We must work on the assumption that men are men irrespective of class or race; and although there are and must be individual differences of race, men must be equal.

That must be the basis of any international organization, if we are to create a sense of security for the common man everywhere in the world.

NC: How do you implement that ideal?

Lange: Well, that's a large order. I think the main thing is to build up an organization with international police power, strong enough to stop any aggressor nation. But it is just as important to create organized cooperation in the economic field in the use of natural resources; also in the social field, with a view to—step by step—and it will be a long way to go—obtaining more equal standards of life among nations. In this, all nations must be prepared to sacrifice what they may consider immediate national interests, to the necessities of international cooperation. Of course these are high ideals, and our generation is rightly skeptical of high-sounding phrases, but we must always realize that such goals can never be reached without sacrifices. And those sacrifices we must, all of us, be prepared to make. Norway will do its bit, modest though it may be. We shall do it by making our own country a better home to live in, and by abstaining, in our foreign policy, from anything that may cause international unrest; also by using whatever influence we may have to further confidence and friendship within the framework of the United Nations.

All our interviewing was done in Lyche's radio studio because our miserable machine was humming louder than ever, and the technicians of Statsradiofonien had no better luck with it than the French, German, American and Danish specialists. So we had no chance to record people in homes, shops, factories, or on the street. But there were others besides cabinet ministers: Gunner Janssen, a sculptor, who said, "I believe the artist belongs, just as much as the scientist, in the forefront of international thinking"; Dr. Otto Mohr, rector of the University of Oslo: "We have to teach people to be able to agree without being disagreeable"; a housewife, Mrs. Halden: "I haven't seen an egg in years. Every now and then I hear them spoken of, but I never hear of them being eaten"; and a treasurable memoir of Evensmo: "I spent two years in a Nazi prison, but I made up for it by becoming the father of twins, nine months from the day of my release."

There was time, on a Sunday, for a free breath, and we took it at Nordemark, a municipal park. People stood, sat or walked with their faces tilted up sharply to the sun. There had been little sunshine all winter and spring, and Oslovians were taking it when they could get it. In the park I was delighted to run into Guri Lie, young daughter of Trygve Lie, whom I had met for the first time only three weeks back, in New York. Nothing collapses the world's distances like a coincidence of two casual meetings, 6,000 miles apart, within days. Well, almost nothing.

Lyche drove us to the airport and we boarded an old Junkers 88 for Stockholm. It was three-motored, with an interior not encountered by me before. A clock and altimeter, set in the door to the cockpit, were on view for all passengers to see. There was also a sliding panel in the cockpit door, and through this the pilot handed a weather report to the nearest passenger. Just an arm coming through the door—as in a spooky movie.

I decided, on this flight, that we are really indifferent students of the atlas, those of us who fancy we are familiar with it. I had looked at a map of Sweden perhaps twenty times in my life, and never really seen the Vanern and Vattern lakes which now lay across our route—great bodies of water, the Vanern being 28th largest in the world—a society that begins with the Caspian and Black Seas and includes the five Great Lakes of America.

We landed at Bromma airport and were met by Dr. James Robbins of the American Legation, Tord Hagen of the Swedish Foreign Office, Sidney Sulkin, CBS's Stockholm man, his wife Edith, and Sven Norberg of Radiotjanst, the Swedish state radio. Dr. Robbins handed me a letter he had been holding for me, postmarked Washington. I opened and read it as we were walking through the airport building.

THE WHITE HOUSE
WASHINGTON

June 15, 1946

Dear Mr. Corwin:

I am glad to see that the concept of
One World, so ably advanced by the late Wendell
Willkie, will be perpetuated through a series of
annual globe-circling flights, underwritten by
the friends of Mr. Willkie.

As the first winner of this award, you
will take with you the best wishes not only of
your colleagues in the arts and sciences, but of
all Americans of good will. Anything which can
promote better relations in a world too long
divided by suspicion and ill will, is of value
to our time.

With my best regards, I am

Very sincerely yours,

Harry S Truman

Mr. Norman Corwin,
Columbia Broadcasting System, Inc.,
485 Madison Avenue,
New York 22, N. Y.

It was a good entrance to Sweden. And it also fortified a sensation that I was back in the United States. For in contrast to the countries we had just come through, Sweden was relaxed and well fed, wanting only adequate fuel—a serious lack in its latitude. High piles of firewood lined some of Stockholm's streets against the coming winter, but otherwise the city seemed as sleek and prosperous as any American metropolis, although more beautiful than most, standing as it does between a sparkling lake and the Baltic Sea.

In the Europe of 1946, it was extremely uncommon to hear a homemaker say she lacked for nothing, yet when I asked an average Swedish mother, wife of a laundry worker, whether she was short of butter, eggs, meat or other commodities, she replied, "I can't say that I miss anything."

Sweden had come by her prosperity through many ways, not the least being her neutrality in two world wars. A modified capitalism, a strong blend of socialism based on a widespread cooperative movement, rich resources, highly developed industries, good management-labor relations, and above all, the luck of having I escaped wars, made her what she was and is.

But in more than standards of wealth and plumbing, did Sweden resemble the United States. Modern American culture was heavily imported. American music, films, periodicals and fashions were subscribed to: newspapers ran pictures of California bathing beauties, along with local news. The comic strip Popeye appeared in the *Aftonbladet,* under the name of Karl Alfred. The week I was there, Karl had an adventure, which ended with his saying, "*Vall ryck mej ocksa!*" ("Well, shake my tail!")

I found that the schoolboy of Sweden had roughly the same ideas and ambitions as the schoolboy of Missouri. I talked one day with twelve-year-old Ove Bergstrom, in a country town near Uppsala. He said he wanted to be a businessman, to travel, to see America, to visit the motor industries in Detroit and the film stars in Hollywood. He had no political opinions, except that Russia was dangerous.

In Sweden, as in America at that moment, Russia was regarded as the crucial element in international relations. I heard a good deal of anti-Russian talk, including the warning that I had better not wear a wristwatch on the streets of Warsaw (our next stop) because Red Army soldiers stationed there would not hesitate to hack off one's wrist in order to get it. Offsetting this was the attitude of the Baroness Erenkrona, a newspaperwoman on the staff of the *Aftonbladet.*

Speaking of Russia, I have an idea—not mine—it comes from many interested people in Sweden, especially the youth—that they would like to get in touch with Russia, because we think that, cost what it may, peace only can be gained by obtaining the confidence of all the people of all nations. We must show Russia our belief in them and not mistrust them; and in exchange, obtain possibly something from the Russian nation to believe in, in our turn.

The prosperity of Sweden was not only industrial. Its agriculture was booming, too. In a farmhouse near the village of Norrby Satery, I interviewed a husky, pink-faced farmer, Sven Siden—whose house looked as though it had been cut out of a fashionable architectural magazine. He was happy with the way things were going, and said his only need was for American tractors, which he preferred to any other kind. He said he was not worried about anything, and I asked whether his confidence included the political situation:

> **Siden:** Yes . . . I don't think I feel what do you call it—(gropes for a word)
>
> **NC:** Nervous?
>
> **Siden:** No. I don't feel nervous about it. I don't think we get another war in my time.

In all countries visited in the flight, most people were eager for a *modus vivendi* to insure existence against the hazards of the atomic age. But nowhere did individuals and government alike show more fervor for peace than in Sweden. It was almost as though the Swedes, having been without war for 140 years, were anxious to stay that way forever. They wanted no war of any description, and to them atomic war was only a refinement. The head of the Swedish Engineering Research Academy, Professor Edy Valander, summed it up in a sentence: "Any kind of war would be catastrophic for us, and I don't think atomic war would be worse than any other."

The women especially seemed to be thinking hard about peace, and I heard all manner of plans, theories, dreams, ideas— some good, some naive, some pathetic, but all very sincere. One plan was that of Mrs. Ludovica Hainlach, who represented a group called The Universalists. She explained that the main point of their program was "realizing our principle, which can be expressed in just two words: 'Mothering the World.'" Then there was the aggressive peace plan of Mrs. Karin Hammar, a twinkling grandmother of 60. She believed that if housemothers of the world united in a great labor union, we might be on our way to unity. She lived in a small town near the industrial city of Bofors, in the center of Sweden.

NC: Wasn't it in Bofors that the famous anti-aircraft guns were made during the war?

Mrs. Hammar: Oh yes, yes. But he's a very peaceful man.

NC: Who is?

Mrs. Hammar: My husband.

NC: Your husband made anti-aircraft guns?

Mrs. Hammar: Yes, yes. But he's a very peaceful man.

NC: Does he prefer that such guns be used to . . .

Mrs. Hammar: Peace all over the world . . .

NC: . . . just to shoot birds with?

Mrs. Hammar: Yes. In the One World. Quite as you, I am also a grandmother.

NC: You're a grandmother?

Mrs. Hammar: Yes, and I have four, er, uh—how you call them?

NC: Grandchildren?

Mrs. Hammar: Four grandchildren!

NC: Mrs. Hammar, what is the name of the organization you represent?

Mrs. Hammar: The Housemothers' Labor Union.

NC: Do you feel you are doing some good?

Mrs. Hammar: Yes, but making peace is not such a dance on roses.

I asked her if she would like to send a message to America, and when she made sure what I meant by consulting a friend, she straightened up and proudly extended greetings:

Mrs. Hammar: I greet all the American housemothers from all my heart and I hope they will be happy and economically independent and they will be able to work for the peace not only in America but in the whole world.

Later there was little, silver-haired 70-year old Kerstin Hesselgren, first woman to become a member of the Swedish Parliament, and a long and stubborn fighter for women's rights:

> Begin with the children. Teach the children from the very first to cooperate and understand and respect each other. Teach the children to respect work, their own work, and to respect other countries as well, and there you have the beginning of the possibility of cooperation among the nations.

Sweden had not yet been admitted to the United Nations, and was anxious to join. In the face of current talk of new power blocs, the acting Foreign Minister, Nils Quensel, indicated precisely where Sweden stood:

> It may take a long time before the United Nations will have become so efficient and stable as is necessary for the very existence of our civilization. It is still conceivable that this attempt at an association of nations will fail and disintegrate in a disastrous Armageddon. In any case I can see no alternative. In my opinion we should join the United Nations with a firm resolution to do our part by making a positive contribution, and to try to counteract the lining up of the powers in different ideological blocs.

Prince Bertil, son of Crown Prince Gustav Adolf, came to the studio at Radiotjanst where I had been interviewing housekeepers and clerks, and, putting at ease the solicitous Swedes in attendance, he proceeded to answer questions as though he had been bred to a microphone.

> **Prince Bertil:** Wendell Willkie used to talk about the great reservoir of good will towards the United States that he found all over the world. I think it is very easy to understand what he meant. When I was in America in 1938, taking part in the tercentenary celebrations of the first Swedish settlements of the Delaware River, I was deeply impressed by the generosity

of mind that is so essentially American. Moreover, I came to understand that it was not an empty phrase when Americans spoke of their country as the New World. You and your forebears, with rugged practical idealism, have been animated by the great dream of building a new community on foundations of freedom and mutual respect. That is, I suppose, why Americans, while building their new world, have never forgotten that they belong to the whole world. It can be no coincidence that the two great attempts of recent history to organize the world for a secure peace, have originated in the United States.

It can never be repeated too often: you have the great reservoir of good will that Willkie spoke of. Don't let difficulties and setbacks discourage you: be patient and stubborn at the same time. The world is in need of the same pioneering spirit that built your own country.

NC: I can only share your hope that my countrymen will stick to the path they have laid out, toward collaboration with other nations, great and small. But don't you think, Your Highness, that the other nations of the world have the same responsibility, and have equally important contributions to make?

Prince Bertil: Of that there can be no doubt. Here, in our own small country, we have tried to develop a community based on social peace, social justice, and a reasonable amount of social security. We are by no means sure that our solutions are perfect, but we have tried and are trying our best. We have learned from other countries, and it is possible that in return, we may have accomplished some things from which others could benefit.

Sweden was the last country where we had to rely on studio equipment for our recordings. When Bland, ready to throw our humbox into the Saltsjo, made one last effort to have the equipment repaired, Radiotjanst's Sven Norberg and Lennart Fablen, who had been delegated to help us around the city and country, reported to Yngve Hugo, Director-General, that we were having trouble with the machine. "Isn't that the very same model we bought from the States last week?" asked Hugo. It was. Hugo insisted that we take their new machine in return for our old and useless one. "What kind of exchange is that?" I protested. "The least we can do is to buy the machine from you and pay what it will cost to have a new one shipped to you from New York." "Won't hear of it." And that was it. We had better luck with this one; it never failed us.

The hospitality of the Swedes was many-sided. Radiotjanst gave us a luncheon at Operakallaren, attended by Prince Bertil, Lord of the Bedchamber Roif Von Heidenstam (that's right, Bedchamber), Minister of Commerce Gunnar Myrdal, known in America for his books on economics and the American Negro, Dr. Robbing, of the Legation, Miss Hesselgren, Mrs. Adele Hehlborn of the American-Swedish Foundation, Sidney and Edith Sulkin, and a large cast from Radiotjanst, headed by Dr. Hugo. Like the Mayor's luncheon in Copenhagen, it was full of toasts and courses, but this time Sulkin briefed me in the etiquette of raising the glass of aquavit, engaging the eyes of the toastee, extending it, giving it a little waggle, returning it to the region of the sternum, elevating it to the mouth, and downing it.

The Americans of Stockholm lived the good life. Dr. Robbins threw a cocktail party on Bellmansgatan to which had been invited representatives of the professions in a cross-section so wide that, if I failed to get a proper perspective of Swedish culture, it was not going to be Dr. Robbins' fault. Among the guests were painters, engineers, composers, actors, producers and directors of the Royal Opera and the Royal Dramatic Theater; the managing editor of *Dagens Nyheter*, the foreign editor of *Dagbladet*, and various educators, including Professor Erik Lindberg, who made medals.

The Sulkins threw a dinner at Hasselbacken. And Helene and Robert Robb, attached to the American Legation, gave a dinner at their apartment, at which I distinguished myself by addressing General Alfred Kessler, Jr., as "Captain," absent-mindedly confusing his rank with that of another officer present. I was not disciplined.

It was the one festive tangent of the whole trip. There were too many Elysian spreads of smorgasbord, too much aquavit, too many clouds of cigar and cigarette smoke to combine comfortably with the rigorous work schedule of the itinerary, so I made a vow to clamp down a curfew if, anywhere else, social life were to beckon quite as urgently. It never did, though we had by no means seen our last dinner party.

Ruined City
Warsaw

*The local devastation is so massive, so utter,
that it defies the senses*

We left Stockholm for Warsaw on a bright, colorless morning,
which bore the good American date of July 4th. We were on the
maiden flight of a new DC-4 Skymaster freshly delivered from
Santa Monica. All the signs and legends on the ship were in English, but the Swedes had painted the name of a girl on each motor:
Margit, Gunvor, Inga-Brjtt and Ingrid.

We crossed a calm Baltic, bisected the island of Gotland,
covered more open sea, and finally made our landfall on the
coast of what was once East Prussia. This territory, now Poland,
was the first along our route, in which we saw any full-scale devastation. Bomb pits and tank tracks were visible from 8000 feet in
the region of Koenigsburg. But not until we approached Warsaw
itself, did we see how ghastly a city can look when it has been
systematically destroyed.

From the air Warsaw was like a painter's imaginary conception
of catastrophe, in which he had overstated his case. No two cities
in the world could provide a more dramatic contrast than the one
we had just left, and the one we had just reached. Stockholm was
beautiful and intact, not a scratch anywhere on its surface; Warsaw

was the most completely destroyed city of the war. The people of one suffered little more than the anxieties of a nervous neutrality. The people of the other suffered anguish beyond record and beyond belief. Little of the harsh detail could be seen in flight; we had to wait until we were on the ground and could view it at eye level to appreciate the extent of the ruins.

We landed at an airport whose only runway had been reclaimed from bomb craters. It was oppressively hot; the flat countryside was parched. We were met by a representative of the Polish Ministry of Foreign Affairs. He greeted us and said, "I am instructed to tell you that you are invited to go anywhere you please in Poland, see anybody you wish, and discuss any subject of your choosing." It so happened that the first place we went was to a July 4th party given by the American Ambassador, Arthur Bliss Lane, in the garden of the Hotel Polonia. Across the street from the hotel stood the shattered main railroad station of Warsaw, its visceral steel framework spewed out, and decaying with rust.

We paid our respects to Ambassador Lane, said hello to Homer Bigart of the *New York Herald-Tribune*, greeted other correspondents, and checked in at the desk. The Polonia was the only centrally located hotel open for business, and it was crowded. Bland and I were quartered a city block apart from each other, in rooms so small we had to stack our suitcases atop the wardrobe, and pull in our midriffs as we passed even that, to get in and out.

There was hardly time to shower and put on a clean shirt, and we were off to a reception, this time Polish, in the garden of the Polish State Radio headquarters. The ride there, in a jeep, was past unending vistas of broken and toppled buildings, burned out homes, twisted debris. The radio station itself was in an old mansion whose blasted interior had been rebuilt since the liberation. Our hosts had learned we were coming only the day before, and had hastily arranged a party to share our celebration of Independence Day. There were good spirits grading up to ebullience, and some of it was captured by our wire recorder:

(Music, shouts in Polish, a voice shouting, "Long live the U.S.A.!")

Man's voice: Mr. Corwin, I know it is the Independence Day today, and though I am just a simple Pole, I'd like to tell you on behalf of all Poles that we like the United States of America very much indeed, and consider the United States to be the greatest country in the world.

(More shouts; cheers)

Then Professor Chizinofsky of the University of Warsaw was introduced and he spoke through an interpreter:

We are children of the great national heroes of both Poland and the United States, Thaddeus Kosciusko and Casimir Pulaski who fell at Savannah. Well, since we're children of these two national heroes, we would like to greet [you] on the Independence Day of the United States of America, on the 4th of July. All the best to the United States of America from all the Poles!

The garden in which these toasts were made was a pleasant oasis among charred and fragmented skeletons of houses in the neighborhood. There seemed to be no point in the city from which the outlook was not one of utter and tragic demolition. Dr. Ignace Zlotowski, a scientist who later became Poland's delegate to the Atomic Energy Commission of the United Nations, explained to me that whereas cities like Berlin and Stalingrad and Manila were devastated by fighting, Warsaw was largely destroyed out of Nazi spite:

About 80 percent of the destruction in Warsaw actually is due to the fact that after the well-known terrible Warsaw uprising, the Germans decided to destroy the city in a very systematic and typically German way. In other words, house by house, street by street. In other words, it wasn't a regular warfare, it was just simple vengeance.

There were artists, writers, musicians, scientists and radiomen at this reception, and uniformly their clothes were plain and worn,

Poland was destitute, it was the first country overrun by Hitler, it endured the longest occupation, it suffered the cruelest treatment. The Poles lost six million dead, of whom three million were Jews. When I was in Warsaw no Pole considered it dishonorable or disgraceful to have a frayed collar, or shoes with holes in them. The Nazis, always bad losers, when it appeared inevitable that they would have to fall back before the next offensive from the east, commandeered as much clothing and furnishings as they could carry, and destroyed the rest. I spent a half-hour interviewing Dr. S. Helsztynski—a good gray poet who is translating American poets, especially Whitman, into Polish.

In spite of the stark gutting of the city, the mood of Warsaw was far from despairing or indolent. Workmen were hacking away at the ruins, by painfully primitive means. They had no tractors, bulldozers, steam-shovels, or acetylene torches. I saw a man cutting a thick steel girder with a 16-inch hacksaw, a task requiring hours. With a torch it could have been finished in a minute or two. Life went on stoically against unbelievable hardships. Families were living and raising children in corners of ruins, which they had cleared of rubble. Students were sharing books. Everybody was busy, including the intellectuals.

Not long before we arrived there had been a national referendum. Signs telling people how to vote were still up on whatever walls were standing. The opposition to the Warsaw Government, led by the Peasant Party of Stanislaus Mikolajczyck, had protested the fairness of the voting procedure, claiming coercion and intimidation. The country was divided—there was an active underground against the government, and sporadic killing and bloodshed over political differences. Charges of terrorism came from both factions; American correspondents themselves differed in estimates of the situation.

What most deeply interested me, as a traveler trying to investigate prospects for One World, was not the claims of either party, but the question of whether the forces which had destroyed Poland in the first place, and killed its millions, were still alive. My questions were mainly to this end.

One day I asked to interview a typical group of Polish workmen, and was taken to a newly reconstructed power plant on the banks of the Vistula. The men were politically conversant. One of them said he did not think atomic energy was the greatest source of power in the world. When I asked him what he did think greatest, he replied, "The human being." Another said he believed the great powers should get together on a definition of democracy before they do anything else. A mechanic asked me to explain Wendell Willkie's concept of One World, and when I did, he said something in Polish that the interpreter translated as follows:

> **Power worker:** I want to say that this idea suits me completely, but I would like to say too, that within this One World every country—for instance, Poland—should be free to have their own possibility to develop their national culture and feeling.

Another worker complained that the Allies were giving more material help to their late enemies than to their recent comrades-in-arms.

> **Second worker:** The thing that is amazing for us is that Italy, a country which fought the Allies, gets more material help than Poland.

I told a third worker that there was an impression in the United States that a substantial part of Poland was unfriendly to Russia. His answer dodged my question:

> **Third worker:** I think we will always work with this nation which will destroy the German power and not this power which will reconstruct. It doesn't matter which power it will be.

What he obviously meant was that Poland would not cooperate with any nation that would reconstruct Germany's capacity; that it didn't matter which nation it was.

The next afternoon we went to Belvedere Palace to record President Boleslaw Beirut. The palace was an expansive white structure, the simplicity and dignity of whose exterior reminded us of our own White House. It overlooked a park whose soft greenness made all the more bitter the ashen wreck of the city that stretched away in all directions. The palace itself survived only because the German high command used it up to the moment it pulled out of Warsaw.

President Beirut was a short, solidly built man with a strong, even a powerful face, a modified Chaplin moustache, the whole softened by a geniality, a warmth, and twinkle of the eye. For a whole hour, sitting at a small table in the Pompeian Room, he talked out answers to my questions before he would permit them to be recorded. Only when be was satisfied that he had given them sufficient thought, did he commit his answers to wire. The full record of this exchange, including the time taken for interpretation both ways, occupied another hour:

> **President Beirut:** The first need of Poland is actually a long last-ing peace between the nations. Only in this way can Poland hope to reconstruct the damage inflicted by war, for it will take us a long time to recover.

He appealed for help to Polish children orphaned by war, for assistance in reestablishing Poland's badly disrupted educational system, and for increased trade between the victor nations. On implementing the peace he said:

> **President Beirut:** The best argument for what collaboration among nations can accomplish in peacetime, is what it accomplished in wartime. Only in One World is it possible to guarantee the future. But in the maintenance of rela-tions between countries one must give thought not only to constructive possibilities, but to the prospective possibilities of a rebirth of the dangers we escaped such a short time ago. I am thinking about the rebirth of Hitlerism and mili-tarism. The gravest danger to us all today is that the democ-racies are not aware of recrudescence of fascism wherever it occurs. In their future collaboration, nations must not forget this danger. Nobody wants a war again.

In most of the other countries of the trip, press conferences were requested by local newspapermen. Sometimes they were set up by the local foreign office, the ministry of information, or the American Embassy. There were the usual questions, so obvious they bear no value here; but now and then, according to the situation, or some indigenous sensitivity, there were especially pertinent or barbed questions. One such conference was held in Warsaw. The Polish newspapermen were particularly interested in whether I had found any "iron curtain"—an index of the degree to which they, in common with the Russians, were smarting from Churchill's coinage of the phrase in his Fulton, Missouri speech of only a few months back. I could answer only that, in my limited travels around Warsaw, I had not.

By July 6, I was so worn out I decided to take a day off, but it was half consumed anyway by visits to the Russian Embassy. Afterward we went to the country, a short distance from Warsaw, where we went through the palace, or one of them, of King Sobieski [the elected king of Poland from 1674–1696, who held back the Ottoman Turks.] We sat in the grass for a while near the idyllic Vistula River. A sudden cool wind broke the torrid heat and was almost chilling. The next day was dull and rainy, so I took advantage of time inside to write a long cable to CBS in New York regarding my interview with Beirut. There was a press conference in the evening. The newspapermen, some of them unkempt, as all Poles have to be these days, what with the destitution of their country by war, they were most friendly, and seemed pleased with my statements. Drank brandy afterward.

Eight American correspondents were staying at the Polonia. One of them, Ruth Lloyd, sister of actor Norman Lloyd, representing the United Press, sat down to Bland's machine and recorded her views on reportage in Warsaw:

> **Lloyd:** There has been no limitation of movement for me here. From the time I arrived, I have been able to go anywhere I pleased, whenever I pleased, and without previous consultation or permission.

NC: Are you free to discuss any subject you please, with anyone?

Lloyd: Yes. On some occasions I was asked to show any quotations that I planned to use, to the person interviewed, to make sure my translations were correct. I find that entirely justified.

NC: Have any of your dispatches been censored by the government?

Lloyd: There has been a lot of talk about censorship. Some correspondents say it exists here. I can only tell you of the case of one correspondent that I know of—Larry Owen of the Associated Press, who claimed that one of his dispatches was delayed for 11 days.

NC: Was it?

Lloyd: The Polish Government said that the dispatch left Warsaw and went to Prague six hours after it was filed, and that it cannot control what happens to dispatches after they leave Warsaw.

NC: Do you mean cables are sent dog-leg from here to Prague? Where do they go from Prague?

Lloyd: To New York. There is one straight RCA circuit to New York, but all routes are highly variable.

NC: I was made to understand by correspondents in the States, that the copy they sent as observers of foreign events was sometimes changed by editors back home. What has been your experience in this respect?

Lloyd: I'm afraid I've had that same experience. I can't speak for anyone except myself. I can only say that a dispatch upon which I expended a great deal of care, in order to make it a most objective report about a very troubled situation here in Poland, was changed almost beyond recognition by the time it hit the American press. The reason may have been that it went through a relay point in Europe before it hit the States, or it may have been rewritten in the States, but when I got the finished copy back, it resembled my copy not at all.

NC: How, specifically, was the sense of the dispatch changed?

Lloyd: Editorially, such things as the insertion of the words "Communist-controlled" before the word "government." And in a reference to the opposition to the government, represented by Mikolajczyck's party, the insertion of the phrase "harried" before "opposition."

NC: Would you say that was exceptional, the kind of thing that might happen once in six months, or is it a chronic hazard awaiting the objective dispatch which doesn't happen to suit the outlook of the editor back home?

Lloyd: Again, I can only speak on the basis of my own experience. But I can say that most of the correspondents fairly well make up their minds before they come here; they know exactly what they are going to find, and they spend the greater part of their time confirming what they hope to find, and ignoring anything else which might upset their preconceived ideas. I find this very unfortunate. (But) as a matter of fact, most of the stories put out by the correspondents here are true. They are based on fact, but sometimes enriched with artistic touches in the telling—a little retouching here and there to obscure the shadows, and help the dispatches to hit the front page.

One day we went with a sound truck into what was left of Warsaw's ghetto. For hours we crawled around and through the rubble of the once walled-in city where the Jews, having lost nearly 300,000 men, women and children to the gas chamber, the oven, the poison pit, typhus, starvation, rallied together, and with pitifully few weapons, stood off a German Army. Twenty-five thousand of them died in minutes; the Nazis placed tanks right up against their houses and fired point-blank. There were hundreds of bodies still buried in those ruins, a sea of ashes and bricks in the silence of a city become a cemetery. Wherever a living thing could attach to earth, weeds grew. But the detail, as we went along, was heartbreaking: a shoe, part of a bureau, some woodwork, an old porcelain bathtub with shrapnel holes through it, a scorched fragment of a Yiddish newspaper. This was not the work of aerial bombs or night-raids in which the defenders had at least antiaircraft guns and a fighter plane or two. This was the fascism that the Poles got to know so much of—with all its cowardice and its sadism. Here was the ultimate picnic ground of the professional anti-Semite; the paradise of Julius Streicher [the editor of the notorious anti-Semitic newspaper, *Der Sturmer*] and the Jew-baiters. This is what they wanted and what they got. I heard more talk about fascists in Poland than in any place I had struck so far. They used the word with special emphasis. Even as we stood there in the ghetto, there was a pogrom in the town of Kielce, 100 miles away; a pogrom which, according to five American correspondents who rushed to the scene, had been coldly and deliberately planned and executed by elements whom the government immediately denounced as hostile to the regime. In any case, Jews—men, women and children—had been ambushed and massacred. [More than 40 Jews who survived Holocaust concentration camps were murdered and 80 more were wounded.]

It was hot that afternoon in the ghetto, hot and still. I looked at a circular stone monument that the city had put up among the debris. Withered and dusty flowers were strewn about. The inscription read, "In memory of those who gave their lives in a singularly heroic fight for the honor of the Jewish people—for liberty—for Poland—for the liberation of all mankind." The monument had been there for a year. But the bodies in Kielce were not yet buried.

Why War?
Soviet Union

"Sit down," said the Chairman, "and tell us about you."

We visited the Soviet Union at a time when relations between that country and ours were badly strained. At home opinion ranged between, at one extreme, a belief that Russia was an unremitting enemy, a tyrannical and backward government which persistently had done nothing but evil within its own borders and in the world outside; and at the other extreme, a belief that she was historically blameless, a true friend of progress, and a glistening new society incapable of doing any wrong. I happened to share neither view, and it was with an open and hopeful mind that I boarded a plane in Warsaw and flew, with Bland and equipment, to Moscow.

We rode on a Lend-Lease DC3, bearing the star of the Red Army, and flown by Red Army pilots. Stenciled on a motor cowling in perfectly good American, was the legend, "Use Filler—Neck Type Oil Heater." There were no safety belts, no food aboard, nothing resembling a steward, and luggage was piled on unused seats. A bicycle was lifted through the passenger entrance, and lashed back in the tail along with bags and suitcases. Thanks to a mystery of currency exchange which baffles me to this day, the fare for Bland, myself, and 350 pounds of luggage, from Warsaw to Moscow, a distance of almost 900 miles, came to $17.66, the result, I was told, of an occluded front between the zloty and the ruble.

For five hours we flew over flat, wooded country. Then suddenly we banked, turned, and came down on an airport, which in size, equipment and activity resembled some of the biggest American civilian airports. Our first inquiry, in hopelessly alien English, brought a tall, quietly dressed executive-looking woman. She was apparently the airport linguist and roving Traveler's Aid. I explained who we were, why we were there, and that, according to advance notices and representations, we were to be the guests of Voks, the Foreign Cultural Relations Society. "Ah," she said, with a look of inspired understanding, "please wait in sitting room." We were led to a spacious, dim and mildly dowdy sitting room, unlike anything I had ever seen in an airport, and the lady said she would immediately communicate with Voks.

It was mid-afternoon. We had the room to ourselves, or perhaps the room had us to itself. I felt a bit quarantined, as we were there for two hours without any visitor or even a person entering the room by mistake. Since at all times on the trip there were never hours enough in any day to keep abreast of reports, note-making, correspondence, the confirming of reservations, and assorted drudgery, Bland and I did not sit around fuming, but instead took over a table in the middle of the room. I tapped out some overdue letters on our little Hermes typewriter, and Bland applied himself to problems of currency, supplies and general logistics.

At length two men from Voks appeared, breathless. They said they had not expected us until tomorrow—that our letters, cables, advices, requests for an agenda of interviews, had arrived in a batch only yesterday. A likely story, considering that the most painstakingly spelled-out statement of objectives, and requests for specific interviews, had been placed with the Soviet consular official in New York, weeks before Bland and I had ever boarded Juan Trippe's airplane.

One of our two airport greeters had been assigned as interpreter and guide for the duration of our stay: Nick Boronin, about 30, with a head of thick, curly hair, clear, frank eyes, an illuminating smile, an economical Slavic nose, quick and hearty humor, but only a fragmentary acquaintance with the English language. Whenever in doubt, he said, "Dot's all right." He used this interchangeably, to mean "maybe" or "I don't understand" or "impossible at such short notice," or "there has not yet been word on your request" or "I'll see what can be done."

He was friendly, cooperative to the extent permitted by his employers, hardworking at whatever he did, never prying, never argumentative, never curious about America, or about where we had been or where we were going. He never asked leading questions or made suggestions; he was honest, direct, affable, discreet, and helpful, and never interposed himself, as zealous interpreters sometimes do, between interviewer and interviewee.

Nick drove us in a Voks limousine over well-paved country roads, which opened, after some miles, onto a wide highway, which in turn led to a heroically broad avenue, which at length skirted the high walls of the Kremlin. Finally we arrived at the Hotel National, next door to the American Embassy. There, after helping us check in, Boronin disappeared, not to be heard from until noon the next day. We were stranded without knowledge of the city, the language, the Cyrillic alphabet, or the hotel restaurant's menu.

However, the National maintained an English-speaking telephone operator and desk clerk, so it was possible to find out that the Hotel Metropole was just a few minutes walk from the National, and to that address we went after dinner to pay respects to Richard Hottelet, then CBS Moscow correspondent. Hottelet had been in the city for months, and it had palled on him. He said the Soviet bureaucracy made working conditions difficult for Western correspondents. It held them at arm's length most of the time, and constantly posed an undeclared threat of *persona non grata*, should outgoing dispatches be considered false or unfriendly to the regime.

In this setting, Hottelet was in no mood to contribute to the agenda of our mission, in the way that CBS personnel had done in London, Paris and Stockholm. There was not much he could have done, since we, as guests of a government agency, had more access to people and places than he. We saw little of him; I think he considered me quite mad for telling a reporter that I thought Moscow was beautiful. But I had just come from a totally wrecked city, and my first sight of the fabulous cathedral of St. Basil on Red Square had somewhat polarized my vision.

I saw the church sitting under a distant cumulus cloud of overwhelming magnificence—a mighty, towering cauliflower head crowned and studded with white, ivory and golden botryoids, the peaks rouged here and there by the rays of a sinking sun. The trunk of the cloud shaded to blues and purples out of the night that was advancing over the plains to the east. This apocalyptic mass sat, excessively and redundantly, on top of the most grandiloquent cathedral in the world, itself an architectural curiosity. I have seen some great skies in my years of looking up and down at clouds, but there never had been one to match that vision of tufts and battlements, that nest of hail and thunder, rising above the vari-colored, spiraling domes and cupolas built for a mad emperor.

We had hoped to be up and about the city early on the morning after we arrived, interviewing the first of a list of 22 people submitted to the Russians through their New York consulate, months before. But Nick was late; we stewed about this, for we had no idea where to reach him. Suddenly he appeared, smiling and without apology. I asked,

"Are we going to begin today?"

"Dot's all right."

"No, I mean will it be possible to record some of the people on the list we submitted?"

"What list?"

It took me ten minutes to explain about the list, and suddenly Nick brightened, "We go to Voks," he announced.

"Are they expecting us?"

He nodded briskly and assured us all was right.

The Voks headquarters was in an unattractive section of the city, but the building itself was prepossessing and comfortable in a deeply capitalist way, like the reading room of the Union Club.

Here we met Eugene Karaganov, blond, short, shrewd, friendly when he warmed up. He said communication had indeed been amiss; and, pouring tea, asked us to bear with Voks while it worked to arrange interviews. It would take several days. It was no easy matter, for it was the dead of summer, and key people were absent from Moscow, just as their opposite numbers leave Manhattan in the heat of July.

I submitted a list, which included 30 items, and with the exception of three, these were accommodated. The three were interviews with Stalin, the composer Shostakovich, and the Soviet commissar of religions. None of these requests was denied in so many words; they simply did not come through. There was some confusion as to whether Shostakovich would be in Leningrad or Moscow; in the matter of the Kremlin, we were invited inside to see museums and churches and the Palace of the Soviets, but not to meet any government spokesmen. It was the only country where we were guests of a government agency that no such contact was made.

In all other respects the Russians were entirely accommodating and gave us a free hand. Although we recorded Russians often at random, we were never required to submit questions in advance, and no attempt was made to censor our recordings. The Russians were certainly aware that upon my return, I could check every last interpretation for accuracy, since the original Russian remained in our possession. If we were followed, as we were forewarned we would be, it must have been invisibly. Our chief trouble was that we had too many evenings without escort and with no knowledge of the city or the language. During our visit we associated with people attached to the American Embassy and with at least one American correspondent known by the Russians to be extremely hostile to the regime. This seemed to have no adverse affect upon the courtesy with which we were treated.

Early in the stay, we asked Nick if he would help us convert American traveler's checks to rubles. "But why?" he asked, "You are our guests. You pay for nothing." I told him that while the gesture was much appreciated, I was traveling as much for CBS as for the Willkie Memorial Foundation, and Bland was traveling *entirely* for CBS. Sorry, Nick smiled, but Voks was host, and insisted it be that way with anybody who came to the country at its invitation—room and meals strictly on the house.

I realized we could do nothing if, when we attempted to pay our bill at the National on leaving, they refused to accept payment. But I found a way around this determined generosity. "Room and board are one thing," I said, "and it would be rude of us to decline your generosity if Voks insists. But we shall have need of hard cash for all manner of incidental expenses, and it would simply not be right for Voks to pay for such things."

"Dot's all right. Such as what things?"

"Oh, just to name a few—taxis, haircuts, something we may want to buy at Gum's Department store, gifts . . ."

"What kind gifts?"

"Well, just this morning I passed a bookstore that displayed beautifully illustrated children's books. I'd like to send half a dozen to the children of friends back home."

Nick nodded, excused himself, and came back shortly with a pile of children's books, and two enormous wads of rubles, which he handed to Bland and me. We protested, but in vain. Finally, rather than embarrass Nick further, we decided to take the bankroll, but as soon as he was beyond earshot, we agreed not to spend a kopek of this money, but to return it as we left the country—a sound plan, because visitors were not permitted to take Russian currency out with them, hence Nick would be forced to receive it back.

Then, in order to make certain that we did not accidentally spend the Voks allowance, we sealed it in envelopes, and took our travelers checks to the American Embassy and converted them through their helpful offices. In the process we met John Davies, Elizabeth Eagan and Manning Williams of the Embassy staff. They were living the usual vacuum-chamber life of foreign diplomats in Moscow—insulated by the Russians from the normal activity of the city, and, on some levels, treated more coolly even than the foreign correspondents. Our friends were full of prophylactic suggestions and hints, such as the caution that if we were apprehended by suspicious police, or got into any kind of trouble in unguided excursions around the city, we should insistently say, "Americans-koe Posolstvo," meaning "American Embassy," or "Voks." Nothing but that. We had occasion to try both of these passwords on an agitated policeman within 48 hours, and neither worked.

At dinner with Embassy personnel next evening, one of the American wives was graphic on the experience of having a baby *a la Russe*, like any Muscovite mother, at a Russian hospital. No anesthesia, and crude facilities. This in a country already distinguished for medical and scientific achievement.

Next morning, Nick did not telephone as he had promised, and this kept us anchored at the National. After a reasonable wait, Bland and I set out for a walk. Within two minutes we found ourselves hard by the tomb of the famous mummy of Red Square, where a long line of pilgrims, as usual, were waiting to see it. I had no desire to view Mr. Lenin, because I have always held death to be the ultimate privacy to which any person is entitled. I know the argument that, having traveled many thousands of miles to this historic square, it was prudish not to look on the face of a man who had changed the history of the world; but my answer is a simple question: If you, Reader, were nearly as famous as God, and could control the disposition of your remains by fiat, would you agree to your mummification so that every Grischa, Piotr and Ivan for generations, including those who were glad you were dead, could gape at you?

The open display of a mummy is a ghoulish form of idolatry, and this goes equally for the revered saints whose necrotic arms, hands, and, occasionally, heads, are to be seen within glass-enclosed caskets as part of the ornamental scheme of certain cathedrals in Germany. Perhaps they are on view elsewhere, but I had seen them only in pre-war Germany, and did not go back afterward to find out if they had come through the bombings safely.

Bland was not keen on visiting the corpse either, so we continued on our walk. But it would have been less trouble had we queued up and taken a turn around the mummy, for within another three minutes we were the center of a tempest. We had been told by Nick, as well as by our American friends, that it was all right to take photographs, providing we did not shoot military installations, airports, bridges, or the usual forbidden subjects. When asked expressly about it, Nick had replied, "Dot's all right"—itself not a definitive answer, but when it tallied with the response we got from others, we were satisfied.

Bland had a little Rolliflex, and since the start had been expedition photographer. As we strolled along the Square he took pictures of St. Basil's, of the mausoleum, of the queue. He then decided to take a picture of the clock tower over the Spassky Gate, and had just clicked the shutter when a policeman, his collar open in a way that would be considered sloppy in an officer back home, apprehended him. The cop waved his hands and barked in Russian.

"Americanskoe Posolstvo," said Bland. That helped not at all. The officer shouted, pointed to the tower, to the camera, to himself, to the camera again, to Bland.

"Voks," I offered.

He stopped, looked at me, decided I was not worth bothering about, and returned to haranguing Bland. His face reddened and he got progressively excited. People had gathered by now and studied Bland and me curiously but not hostilely. I had visions of landing in jail, an unscheduled stop that would comment wryly on the One World mission. What a dispatch it would make for Hottelet!

"Americanskoe Posolstvo," I said, a little louder.

"Voks!" snapped Bland, losing his calm.

The officer was now in quite a passion, noisier than ever. Suddenly Bland got an inspiration. He thrust the Rolliflex under the officer's nose, wound the remaining unexposed negative through to the end, unfastened the back of the camera and plucked out the roll of film. The crowd watched, surprised and speechless, as Bland sealed the spool with a tab of gummed paper, slapped it in the officer's hand and walked off. The officer turned the spool over and over, as though he had never seen anything like it before.

Some of the kibitzers pressed closer to see what he held in his hand; the rest went on their way, as did I. No attempt was made to follow Bland or me, to find out who we were in case the film, when developed, might show military installations or secret documents.

Certainly the time on the clock of the Spassky Gate tower was not classified information, but the cop did not know this then, nor did he know that the most innocuous tourist scenes were on the first three or four negatives. We expected to be pursued as we walked with exaggerated casualness back toward the National, but nobody bothered us, and the policeman was swallowed up in the anonymity of the Russian masses.

Nick arrived at the hotel, cheerful and innocent, in mid-afternoon. He had been working hard on arrangements for recording, and had forgotten that he said he would call. When we told him what happened in Red Square, he listened gravely. He could not explain the cop, but said that if we had been able to communicate there would have been no trouble. A measure of Nick's and Voks' eagerness to please us was indicated by the way they compensated for anything we found less than satisfactory. Thinking that the net effect of the incident was to frustrate our picture-taking, Nick, without telling us in advance, arranged for a professional photographer to go about town with us the next morning, taking whatever shots we wanted, and a great many more.

Later in the stay, when I mentioned to Nick that a meeting held earlier with Moscow Radio Committee had yielded less of an exchange of ideas than I had hoped, he set up a second such evening in the conviction that the second one would do better. I tried to dissuade him, but he was adamant. I learned not to report any reservations about our experiences to Nick. Russian hospitality, as many another visitor has found, is as open and vast as the country itself, and sometimes can be overwhelming. Nick, even though a minor government worker, had it in princely measure, and so did his superiors at Voks.

Bland and I were invited to luncheon by U.S. Ambassador and Mrs. Walter Bedell Smith, at Spaso House, a palace built by a millionaire merchant of the Czarist days, and, like most of the palatial outcroppings of Europe, a splendid thing. General Smith had come to Moscow after being Eisenhower's Chief of Staff in Europe, and having headed the Allied delegation that accepted Germany's surrender. He had not been long in Russia, and was ailing. He was late in joining the enormous round luncheon table, and looked drawn and weary. He said little, seemed in pain, and excused himself early. There were only six at the table besides Ambassador and Mrs. Smith: Bland, myself, a Captain Allen, one of the two Cochrans of the State Department, and two other civilian Americans whose names I failed to get. It never ceased to amaze me that the world is such a small precinct; Mrs. Smith recalled meeting me at a reception given by Major Ralph Forster of Canada, in Washington a year before. For an enclave isolated in the heart of a basically suspicious and aloof city, there was reasonably good cheer at the table, thanks to the warmth and buoyancy of Mrs. Smith. Those American movies, which depict tentative and helpless helpmates of foreign-service diplomats, would do well to model them after the General's wife.

From luncheon we returned to the National, were picked up by Nick and a recording truck, and drove to the Park of Culture and Rest, at the edge of the Moscow River. Here were hundreds of children, most of them barefooted, dressed poorly but in good health and spirits, enjoying facilities that I had never seen in children's playgrounds elsewhere—a row of doll houses, a miniature shooting gallery, fountains in whose basins kids could play, large rocking chairs on which tots propelled themselves back and forth.

Then incongruously, a band-less bandstand, and even more incongruously, a soprano and baritone, accompanied by a pianist, taking turns singing arias from Russian operas. A speaker solemnly introduced each number, like Milton Cross guiding listeners through an opera broadcast. The children listened with hushed interest. There was none of the fidgeting or inattention one would expect at such a recital from an audience of children ranging from six to 14 years of age. We recorded some enchanting kids, one of whom was studying English. Did she know any American songs? I asked. She complied:

Good morning, good morning, good morning to you
Good morning, good morning, we are glad to see you.

Cultural exchange. Every little bit helps.

That night Nick took us to the first of the two encounters with the Radio Committee. We entered a solemn oak-paneled conference room, where a group of ten received us. Its chairman stepped forward. "Sit down and tell us about you," he said, immediately. It was blunt and businesslike. Through Nick, I detailed the objectives of the One World trip, the American brand of idealism that it served, and some of the techniques that would go into the ultimate production of the program based on our worldwide recordings. They seemed bored by all this, and showed interest only in the wire recorder, a type which none of them had ever seen. "You Americans!" said one admiringly, as he examined the machine.

Next day our recording activity went into high gear for the first time since we reached Moscow. In the morning we drove to a collective farm only seventeen kilometers from the heart of the city. I had heard much of Russian collectives, and had an idea they were immaculate and highly automated. This one, at least, was far from that. Its 215 people lived in 94 ramshackle houses, making up a village; the farm buildings were run down; I could see no modern machinery about, but was told that tractors and other equipment were interchanged among neighboring collectives in order to get maximum use from them. This particular collective had distinguished itself by increasing production; in potatoes alone the yield from the same ground had been increased 500 percent since before the war.

We went first to the office of the collective, and met its middle-aged chairwoman, Mrs. Olga Petroven. Like almost every Russian we met, she had lost someone in the war—in her case, a brother who was killed on the Leningrad front. I asked her how many men from the farm entered the services, and she answered, "During the war they have taken 130 young men into the Red Army and seven girls; and after the war only 40 men returned, and four girls."

It was a shocking statistic, and underscored the impression we had already formed on the streets of Moscow: that Russia was far more deeply wounded in the war than was generally understood in America. We saw more maimed and blinded veterans there than in all the other cities of our journey, put together. Hardly a family in the 16 Republics had escaped from the war unscathed. As for the universal dowdiness and drabness of the clothes in both city and country, I took these to be badges of honor, their cotton and wool and rayon having gone to higher uses. Where in the States, disruptions of normal civilian life had been mostly a matter of inconveniences—rationed sugar, a scramble for airplane-seat priorities, blacked out waterfronts, a browned-out New York City for a short time—in Russia there had been invading armies, scorched earth, starvation, disease, the gallows, the bestiality of Nazi occupation, and, topping all, thirty million dead.

I asked Mrs. Petroven if I could talk to one of the returned veterans. She sent a boy out into the fields to fetch Ivan Nicolai Suchotin, a 41-year old sergeant who fought on the Leningrad front, and later was wounded in the offensive that carried to Berlin. He told me he was married, had four children, and had lost a brother in the defense of Stalingrad. I asked him what he thought the world had learned from all this fighting. His answer was quick and ready in Russian, but as it came from Nick the interpreter, I'm afraid it lost something in eloquence:

> His opinion about the war: He tells that the Soviet Union, we didn't want to have war as we had with Germany [*sic*] government, and now nobody wants to have the war, and he says that I may say for everybody that nobody in the Soviet Union and I think in the world, she wants the war.

To this statement, Mrs. Petroven requested permission to add her own:

> I send greetings. First of all, I want to tell all the peoples over the world must be friends. They must be good friends and I don't want and nobody wants to see such a great war as we had with fascist Germany. All the people over the world in other countries are good friends and nobody wants to lose so many people as we did in this war. I ask you to say to your people, to the people of the United States and all other countries, best regards from this collective farm.

In its crude simplicity, in earnestness unprompted by any official government line, this sentiment came from all Russians to whom Bland and I spoke. It was the theme of our five hours on that farm. Something of the sense of dedication that has been instilled in the children, came in our recording of 15-year-old Sura, more formally known as Alexandra Suchotin, same name, but no relation to the veteran. She was the daughter of one of the farmers, and when she learned that visitors from America had arrived, she ran home and got into her best dress. I asked her what she wanted to be when she grew up:

Sura: A doctor.

NC: A medical doctor?

Sura: Yes, medical doctor.

NC: Why do you want to be a doctor?

Sura: It would help the Red Army.

NC: Any other reason?

Sura: It would be very useful for our people in the Soviet Union.

NC: You know that it's going to be a long, hard job to become a doctor? You have to study for years and years.

Sura: I know it perfectly and I'm not afraid of it. We are not afraid of hard work at all.

That alone would make Sura sound like a little minion of the state, but actually she was delightfully girlish, full of enthusiasm for music and camping and volleyball and movies. She told me her favorite subject in school was the Russian language; her favorite author Pushkin, her favorite sport, volleyball. Her favorite American picture was *The Great Waltz.* She was fond of musicals; had seen a Russian musical film three times, and memorized one of the hit songs. This with a little coaxing, she sang for us. I asked her if she would like to send a message to children of other countries: "I want to see all the children of the world to be gay and joy[ous] as we are in the Soviet Union."

The farmers took us for a tour of the fields—nothing much after Wisconsin and the San Joaquin valley, but enough to help feed the population of an area covering a sixth of the globe. Then we were led to a small log cabin, one of the old fairy-tale log houses that pass like motes across the mind's eye when you read the phrase "Mother Russia" in Russian novels.

It was tidy inside. An enormous, pregnant bed, piled high with bedclothes, presented itself on entering. Then a kitchen that combined as a dining room and living room. An icon in one corner. A great table sagging under food and drink—fish, black bread, garlic, sausages, cheese, hardboiled eggs, curds and whey, pickled cucumbers, black caviar, smoked salmon, and vodka. As soon as the dishes were uncovered all the flies in the Soviet Union swooped down on them.

The farmers drank a great many toasts to the happiness and friendship of both our countries; they were offered humbly and sincerely. A dozen farmers were around the table, including those we had interviewed, and little Sura. Their genuine affection for America was unexpected and moving. It was as though diplomatic relations between our countries were off in another world entirely, as though these people had never heard (or if they had heard, never cared) about the veto, the atom bomb, the charges and counter-charges in the headlines.

Back we went to the city to meet composer and musicologist Gregory Schneerson, and with him as interpreter, we paid a visit to Aram Khatchaturian at his apartment in a building that housed 55 members of the Society of Composers. It was the sort of studio apartment one might find in the old roomy buildings in New York City.

Khatchaturian, then 43, was just beginning to show gray in his black, wavy hair. He was in shirtsleeves, his collar open, the knot of his tie slipped down. His heavy eyebrows, slightly bulging brown eyes, un-retiring nose and full mouth, combined to give him an earthy yet exotic quality, quite in character with his music.

His wife, Nina Makarova, was pleasantly buxom, her Slavic good looks accentuated by modesty of manner and dress. She wore a simple white, dotted cotton blouse, softly ruffled at the neck; her black hair was parted in the middle, and braided across the front. We started talking about the apartment:

Khatchaturian: The whole building is a gift from the State to the Union of Soviet Composers.

NC: Does that mean a composer doesn't have to worry about where his rent is coming from? Or whether his work will sell, or earn royalties?

Khatchaturian: No, no, no, that is not a problem.

NC: Do you get along well together, or do you tend to avoid each other's society?

Khatchaturian: On the contrary, we like to be together. We discuss and criticize our work, we sometimes eat together, play volleyball together, we even go to each other's concerts.

NC: No jealousies?

Khatchaturian: Why?

NC: Competitors in the same business.

Khatchaturian: Nonsense. What comes out of our closeness is not antagonism but new ideas. We get a lot of work done.

The composers union, it developed, maintained a fund of millions of rubles, had its own medical program, a publishing outlet, and special services such as a community tailor and shoemaker. I asked Khatchaturian about the economics of Soviet music. He said composers were commissioned by the Committee on Arts, with a collective eye to the individual's style and talent. Theme and treatment were not forced upon him, but were left to him to suggest. The going fee for a symphony was 10,000 rubles—about $2000—as a sort of advance, but not against royalties, which accrued to the composer from performances both at home and abroad. Pensions and sick benefits came in the package.

I asked Khatchaturian on what he was working. He said that within the last 18 months be had written the score of a film named *Girl Number 217*, staged his *Gayne Ballet*, written an overture, and was finishing a cello concerto. Then he remembered:

Khatchaturian: Just a few weeks ago, I finished three big arias for soprano and orchestra.

NC: What, an opera?

Katchaturian: No, not an opera. Songs written on a classical text. I've dedicated them to my wife. She composes too.

NC: Two composers in the family? Does that make for any difficulties?

Khatchaturian: There are some complications, but it's a joy.

NC: Is she your best friend and severest critic?

Khatchaturian: My first critic, and my most valuable.

NC: What about actual procedure? Do you audition work in progress for her? Do you discuss the themes and development as you go along?

Khatchaturian: Yes. Absolutely.

NC: Is your cello concerto scheduled for performance?

Khatchaturian: Not yet, but already all the cellists in Moscow are contesting who will be the first to perform it.

NC: All actors want to play Hamlet. Does the concerto, like so much of your work, draw upon your native Armenian background?

Khatchaturian: Well, I never think about it consciously, but it's in my blood, and I suppose it is always reflecting itself in my music.

NC: Is Nina Makarova working on a new composition right now?

Khatchaturian: Yes, that's right.

Makarova: An opera.

NC: Now, do I call you Miss Makarova or Mrs. Khatchaturian?

Schneerson: She is Miss Makarova. She is well known as the composer Nina Makarova.

NC: Supposing both of you have a fit of inspiration at the same time, who gets the use of the piano first?

Makarova (laughing): We have five pianos.

NC: *Five?*

Makarova: Yes.

NC: Now if every composer in this building has five pianos, it would mean almost 300 pianos. That would sound pretty exciting if they all got going at once.

Khatchaturian: There are very many pianos, but not 300. In each apartment there are at least two. I think Soviet musical culture is very high.

NC: Of course there is the classic definition of culture according to the Nazis. One of them said, "Whenever I hear the word culture, I reach for my gun."

Khatchaturian: That war that just ended was not only a war of tanks and guns, but a war of cultures. On one side was the great culture of the United Nations, on the other, the culture of barbarians, degenerates and sadists.

NC: Some correspondent said recently that the art of this country is in as low a condition as its material comforts. Would you comment on that?

Khatchaturian: Some people judge a culture by the condition of an apartment, by the things you have and use in everyday life. I say that real culture is spiritual, not material. I will not deny that the comforts of living are important, but there have been too many classic examples to prove that one need not be comfortably situated to express genius. I'm not against comfort, but it's not everything. My father lived in only one room. Together with my wife, I have six. I hope my little son will have twelve.

I asked him whether he would play something from his cello concerto that I could record. He complied amiably by singing the cello part of the slow movement while Nina Makarova paraphrased the orchestral accompaniment on one of their five pianos. When they finished, Khatchaturian laughed and said, "Playing one's work in public is like reading your own letters in a divorce court."

Moscow at this time in its history was not, all things considered, an attractive capital. Outside of the Kremlin, which bore to it the same relationship architecturally, esthetically, and politically that the Forbidden City did to Peking, there was little to suggest that it was the first city, the control center, the cultural nexus of all the Russians. Like the art of painting under Stalin, it was prudish, proper, and reactionary. Nothing as adventuresome as even the old Flatiron Building in New York. If Moscow ever graduates from being a barracks for its people, it could, with its nucleus of the Kremlin, its compatible river and its gentle hills, become a capital for tourists as well as for the sociologically curious.

I found more than enough time to contemplate these and other matters on the day following my visits to the collective farm and the Khatchaturians. I suddenly came down with a flaming sore throat and high fever, diagnosed as a streptococcus infection. It completely disrupted my recording schedule. But the interviews Nick had arranged were too valuable to lose, so I briefed Bland on questions to ask particular people, and he went out in the Voks truck with Nick Borodin and an assistant, Eugene Umnov, to meet, first, Sergei Eisenstein, greatest of the Soviet film makers.

Photographs taken of Eisenstein in this interview show him in pajamas, arms akimbo, looking not quite recovered from his recent heart attack. At this time, thanks to one of those loopy meanders in the turgid stream of Communist policy on the arts, Eisenstein was under somewhat of a cloud of official displeasure.

The interview took place in the garden of Eisenstein's two-story dacha, a seven-room house set among noble pine trees. In the course of the talk a housekeeper brought some cookies, wine, and tea. Eisenstein asked to be excused from drinking wine because of his health, and indicated that he might have to live in pajamas for another six months or so. Bland reported that he found Eisenstein charming, warm and cordial. "I was intrigued by his bright, dancing eyes—incongruous for a sick man."

When asked to pose for a picture with the dacha in the background, Eisenstein declined, ascribing his reluctance half-jokingly to a superstition about being photographed in or before the house.

He proposed instead that they go to the edge of some woods, which bordered the house. On their way they encountered a horse, and Bland suggested they get the horse into the picture. Eisenstein again declined, and made a running joke of it—the viewer might be confused as to which was himself and which the horse—and if the horse should turn its back to the camera, Eisenstein's Hollywood friends might read some wry commentary into it.

Bland: Mr. Eisenstein, your many admirers in America will want to know your plans, what you are working on at present, and when you intend to visit the States again.

Eisenstein: Well, I am very pleased to hear that there are still Americans who remember me. I was always a great enthusiast of Soviet-American friendship that started from the beginning when I visited the United States in 1930, and I hope that the friendly relationship we had then will resume after this period when it is not too friendly.

Bland: I share your hope.

Eisenstein: I am very pleased to hear that from an American. So you are interested to know what I am doing at the present time. Well, for the last six months I have lived in pajamas, since my heart attack last February. This stopped my work on *Ivan the Terrible*—the second part is still unfinished. There remain to be done a couple of small sequences, which I hope to finish this fall. I use my time—and I have a lot of it now—in working on two of my books, which continue the line of theoretical questions, which I started to develop in *The Film Sense*. This was published in the States during the war. That takes nearly all my time.

Bland: When are you coming over again?

Eisenstein: Well, it's difficult to say. It depends not only on my work, which will take a lot of time, but also, and even more importantly, on the atmosphere of friendship which will prevail between our countries. I don't want to visit a hostile America.

Bland: Would you care to elaborate on that a little further?

Eisenstein: Well, if you insist I can give you certain details about it. When I visited the States in 1930, I had a certain foretaste of hostile people, and of their attitude toward myself and my country. . . . There was a certain native priest [Father Charles Coughlin] at that time who was later at the head of a pro-fascist movement, and he was trying to make all possible difficulties toward my stay there. I would prefer, on a visit, to be free from all this disagreeable kind of thing. I do not like to be bossed around when I have the pleasure of visiting a marvelous country.

Bland: Mr. Corwin's next question, Mr. Eisenstein, is whether you feel that the cinema internationally has been of ample service to the causes of peace and democracy?

Eisenstein: I wouldn't say that. Much more could be done . . . I think your people can work in the direction of showing more themes of unity, understanding and goodwill in your movies. The only counterbalance to all the terrible things threatened by the atomic age, lies in unity and understanding of peoples, even if pressures must be put on governments. Movie people, no less than others, have to be honest, and not hide their true feelings. Act, I say. Time is short. It is not discussion but action that must be taken. If people don't start soon, it will be too late.

More discussion along these lines, then:

Bland: What do you consider to be the ten greatest films of all times?

Eisenstein: I think one of the greatest films of all times is *Birth of a Nation* by Griffith, although I have a quite different view on the question of the colored people as they are presented in the picture. But from the standpoint of pure art, it is certainly a masterpiece. Then I would mention not one, but *many* films by my great friend Charlie Chaplin, whom

Corwin receives a delivery of fan mail from CBS secretary Sally Austin in the early 1940s.

Corwin and Frank Sinatra backstage at Madison Square Garden, Dec, 6, 1945, at the Newspaper Guild "Page One Awards." Both were recipients.

Corwin accepts the One World Award at the Waldorf Astoria.

Norman congratulated by Mrs. Wendell (Edith) Willkie and Bill Paley.

(from left) Charles Laughton, Paul Robeson, Corwin, and Robert Young at the Beverly Wilshire sendoff.

Corwin and Lee Bland leaving LaGuardia, June 15, 1946.

Corwin arrives in Gander, Newfoundland, the first stop.

Corwin with Vladimir Hurban, the Czech Ambassador to the US.

Paris, France
20 June, 1946

Dear Tommy:

      I flw by airplane from London today, abd
it was a great thrill to cross the Englim channell over
ꭗx whichso much of he fighting was done in the
war.
      I will have a busy time of it in Paris, and
I'm not sure whetherI will choose to go from here
to Brussells, which is the capital of Belgium,
or to Copenhagen, in Denmark.
      Tell your dad and mom that I interviewed
Mr. Atlee, tixxp the prime minister of England,
yesterday, and that I also interviewed Sir Alexander
Fleming, who discovered penicillin.
      Also tht Lonꝺ n was very cold and rainy, and
that Paris is much warmer. Tell yoἱr Dad also that
I trɯt he remembers the Hotel Du Bac. I am staying
in a much more fashиonable place, called the Grand
Hotel. The Paris Conference is on at the moment, so
the place is crowded.
      Cigarettes from America cost $1.40, which is
a½good reason, if one were needed, not to smoke.
      Give my love to everybody,

                                  Uncle Norman

C.B.S.
PARIS
Corwin

AR AVION

Thomas Corwán, Esq.
8690 Vista ꭗxꭗꭗ Grande
West Hollywood, 46,
California
UnitedSx States of America

PAR AVION   AIRMAIL

Corwin took the time to send a letter to his eight-year-old, stamp-collecting nephew
Tommy from each stop of the One World Flight.

Left: Corwin with Prince Bertil of Sweden.

Below: Bland and Corwin arrive in Warsaw.

Corwin with his interpreter in the ruins of Warsaw.

Corwin in the Warsaw Ghetto.

Warsaw, Poland
July 5, 1946

Dear Tommy:

This city is the perfect horrible example of
what fascism can do. By the time you are old
enough to see Warsaw for yourself, it will, I hope,
have been rebuilt. But it may take a generation
to get this desolated city and this
impoverished country back on its feet.

I arrived yesterday, July 4th, and stepped
into broiling heat after the coolness of Sweden.
From now on through China, I imagine it
will be hot. But I have two summer suits
and a lot of sleeveless shirts.

Tell your Dad to copy my letters and send
them home for the Round Robin.

Love to everybody,

Uncle Norman

Corwin's letter to nephew Tommy

Reception for Corwin given by Polish Radio.

A picnic in Warsaw with UP correspondent Ruth Lloyd, American radio journalist Arthur Gaeth and unidentified man in background.

Left: Corwin near St. Basil's Cathedral in Moscow, July 1946.

Below: Corwin interviews a woman in the office of a collective farm in Russia. Interpreter Nickolai Boronin is seated between them.

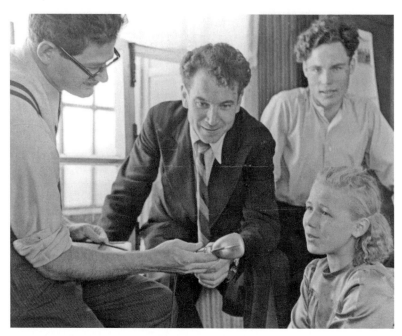

Corwin, Boronin and young woman and man from Russian collective farm.

Corwin visits a Russian commune.

The literary forum discussion of *On a Note of Triumph* in Moscow.

(from left) Nina Makarova, Corwin, Boronin, Gregory Schneerson, and Aram Khatchaturian at the Society of Composers house.

Bland and Sergei Eisentstein

Charm and chat with unidentified women

Above: (from left) Nick Boronin, Corwin, and Bland in Moscow Subway

Left: Corwin's letter to nephew Tommy

Mockba
CCCP
11 July, 1946

Dear Tommy:

Mockba is the way the Russians spell Moscow, and CCCP is how it looks in Russian when you write USSR, which saxxx means Union of Socialist Soviet Republics. You will find out all about the Soviet Union when you begint axx to study modern history in school,---orbefofe then, if you ask your Dad and Mom.

This is a great city of about 6 million, and it has a subway which is more elegant than some our art museums at home. In fact it is the only really clean subway I have ever seen. The streets in many places are about three times wider than Sunset Boulevard, and the squares are big enough to hold a small town in them.

There is some talk about flying to Leningrad during my stay in the USSR, to see the great composer Shostakovich. You will hear a lot of his music when you are older. Maybe I can get him to play something from one of his new works.

Give my love to everybody,

Uncle Corwin

Cowin interviews Czech President Eduard Benes while Bland records.

I admire very much. The third place I give to the Mickey Mouse cartoons, which I consider one of the greatest contributions of the American people to the world. I also like a film by John Ford, *Young Mr. Lincoln,* probably because I am a great admirer of Lincoln himself. Then Lillian Hellman's *The Little Foxes.* And I would certainly include *Citizen Kane* by, er, by . . .

Bland: Orson Welles . . .

Eisenstein: Exactly. I think I had forgotten his name for a moment because he recently wrote something lousy about the first part of my book. I would be very pleased if you would see that this gets back to him. (Laughs).

Of the four men Nick had arranged for us to interview, I had been especially keen to meet Sergei Prokofiev. I had always gone for his blend of Russian sturdiness and vigor with Gallic wit and astringency. Together with millions of his public, I admired the daring of his orchestral color, the rich melody, the lyric flights, the exciting locomotive rhythms. He seemed to me a Slavic Chabrier, with tinctures of Rimsky and Stravinsky; still, not in the least derivative. But it was not for me to meet him. It was for Bland.

Prokofiev received Bland at his dacha forty miles outside Moscow, a big house painted yellow, cream and white, standing, like Eisenstein's house, among tall pine trees. It had a gambrel roof, arched dormer windows and railed porches, with enough windows on the lower level to look out on a Bay of Naples.

Prokofiev's neighbors, composer Nikolai Miaskovsky, and the musicologist Paul Lamm, were present also. The Prokofievs had been in the house only ten days, and not all of the furniture was installed. Prokofiev preferred that the recording be done on the sun deck; the rooms inside, he felt were uncomfortably bare. He was nattily dressed in a gray tweed suit; Miaskovsky, wearing a distinguished gray beard, was dressed in a cap, sports coat and dark slacks.

Bland began by asking Prokofiev what he had been writing. Like Khatchaturian, his music was being played everywhere. Four major works had been performed in Moscow the previous season: his Fifth Symphony; the score for Eisenstein's *Ivan the Terrible*; an opera based on Tolstoy's *War and Peace* and the ballet *Cinderella*. The film score had been written in an interval between the first draft and the orchestration of his Fifth Symphony. During rehearsals of his opera, he undertook a violin sonata.

> **Prokofiev:** Now I'm working on the Sixth Symphony, two movements of which are ready. Also the violin sonata. It's real funny—in America was performed first my second (violin) sonata, which was finished before the first. (Laughs) The first will be ready in a month, I believe.
>
> **Bland:** Why did you start with the second rather than the first?
>
> **Prokofiev:** No, I started the first, then interrupted work on it and began the second. Still, the first keeps its number. I'm doing more work on the *Cinderella* ballet, and a suite of waltzes. Altogether four works will be finished next week, ready for the start of the fall season.
>
> **Bland:** That's wonderful news for your American admirers.
>
> **Prokofiev:** Too much Prokofiev, I'm afraid.
>
> **Bland:** There can never be too much. When are you coming back to the States for another visit?
>
> **Prokofiev:** Certainly as soon as possible. I have been to America several times, and was accustomed to going there every two or three years, but it has been eight years since my last visit, and I'm very eager to see again America, and my friends there.
>
> **Bland:** By the way, have you seen Walt Disney's treatment of *Peter and the Wolf*?
>
> **Prokofiev:** No, unfortunately I have not seen it. I remember my talk with Walt Disney when I was there in 1938, but he was not yet ready to do it then. I saw only a few pictures of the movie in *Life*.
>
> **Bland:** What do you think of our contemporary American composers?

Prokofiev: I am very sorry, I don't know what they have been doing the last eight years, but I liked Gershwin a great deal, particularly his opera *Porgy and Bess.* I liked it very much.

Bland: As a member of the Soviet Society of Composers, have you freedom to write in whatever idiom you wish?

Prokofiev: Certainly. Nobody orders me [to do] anything—and I think what I want.

There are musicians who believe Miaskovsky was greater than Prokofiev, and among the greatest Russian composers of all. In any case, Miaskovsky spoke into Bland's machine—in Russian, since he did not, like neighbor Prokofiev, speak English (yet he was inspired by English texts, having composed symphonic poems based on "Silence," after Poe, and "Alastor," after Shelley). Schneerson translated. The discussion opened with a reference to the fact that Miaskovsky was then at work on his 25th symphony.

Bland: That's quite a number of symphonies. How do you account for having written so many?

Miaskovsky: I never write anything but symphonies and chamber music. I have never written any operas or film scores.

Bland: Who do you consider the most promising young composers in the Soviet Union today?

Miaskovsky: Several who are already quite well known in America, like Kabalevsky and Khrennikov.

Bland: What is your opinion of American composers?

Miaskovsky: I don't know very much about American music. I'm sorry about that. But of what I do know, I think very highly of Roy Harris, Aaron Copland and Samuel Barber. Also I was greatly impressed on hearing a recording of *Porgy and Bess.* I consider George Gershwin a really great composer.

Bland: Is the reason you have heard so little of American music because you have been busy composing symphonies, or because not enough American music is sent to the Soviet Union?

Miaskovsky: The second reason. American music is not much performed here. Whatever American music reaches us goes mostly to the libraries and not into private use.

Bland: Would you like to have more access to American music?

Miaskovsky: Yes, certainly, I am most anxious to have it.

Bland: Would you care to comment, Mr. Miaskovsky, about freedom of art in the Soviet Union?

Miaskovsky: There is no question about that. We write whatever we like.

Bland then asked the usual question about the musician's responsibility to the world beyond his artistic sphere, and how they could best interrelate. The answer was similar to that given by his colleagues.

Alas for these protestations of free rein, all of which I am sure were sincere, the government soon after frowned on its best composers for "formalism," one officially-inspired periodical going so far as to charge Shostakovich with representing an "extremely dangerous tendency toward pathological naturalism, eroticism, and formalistic perversion." Khatchaturian, and, to a lesser degree, Prokofiev, also felt the regime's displeasure. Not that they were banned from writing, or had their drivers' licenses suspended; but they were warned to be more careful.

Bland, on his rounds of suburbia, also recorded Russia's foremost scientist. Peter Kapitza lived only five minutes from Prokofiev, near the Institute of Physical Problems, of which he was the director, in a home that the government had built for him. His property was enclosed by a substantial wire fence about seven feet high, and the Voks bus carrying Bland and Nick stopped at a gate where guards were stationed. They opened the gate before Bland and Nick and closed it behind them, a procedure Bland felt was clear indication that Kapitza was engaged in some important government work requiring protection and precaution.

At the time of this visit, neither Bland nor I, having small expertise in science, was aware of Kapitza's extraordinary background and accomplishments. In the Cavendish Laboratory, he was one of the scientists who first succeeded in splitting the atom; became the first foreigner in 200 years to be elected a Fellow of the British Society; undertook a full Professorship at Cambridge; and in 1934 went back to Russia to attend an international scientific conference in the company of colleague Niels Bohr, the great Danish physicist. Kapitza was treated cordially, but there was only one hitch: he was not permitted to leave Russia and return to his family and laboratory in England. The Soviets wanted him to stay and help. He was understandably nettled; so was Lord Rutherford, who appealed to the British government to intercede. Scientists around the world protested, but Russia held on to Kapitza, cajoled and courted him, offered to build whatever facilities he wanted and to take care of him in style. They put up a fine home for him and his family, placed two chauffeured cars at his disposal, and saw to it that black caviar was in good supply. He eventually thawed out, and became extremely valuable to his kidnappers.

A single Kapitza innovation—the introduction of liquid oxygen to high-temperature processes in the manufacture of steel, brick and petroleum, is credited with having fabulously reduced the amount of fuel needed in these operations—in one case (the making of brick) by 60 percent. My ignorance about Kapitza was obviously not shared by American science, for two years earlier he had been awarded the medal of the Benjamin Franklin Institute, and in the year of our interview, was elected to membership in the American National Academy of Science. His discovery of the superfluidity of helium alone would have made him a celebrity in the society of science.

Bland found Kapitza to be a well-padded man of medium height with affable blue eyes and light brown hair worn with the carelessness typical of scientists. He spoke very good English, and his voice was very much like that of the actor Nigel Bruce. He was dressed in easy-going tweeds.

> **Bland:** Professor Kapitza, would you be good enough to tell me what is the position of the scientist in Soviet Russia?

Kapitza: Our scientists are regarded on the basis of the cultural and social development of our country; therefore the position of the scientist is one of great importance.

Bland: Do you think there *may* one day be cooperation between Russian and American scientists?

Kapitza: It is not only possible but will one day be necessary. The obstacles that separate people and government—obstacles of economy and social theory—can be surmounted. In science, just as in living, when a postulate is proven correct, the truth of it can be shown in many different ways. The same applies to the fundamental principles of life: if our objectives and idealistic goals are similar, then the way we achieve them need not be identical, so long as we both arrive at the same destination. In other words, we need not get involved in irreconcilable contradictions.

Bland: What are your views on the constructive peacetime uses of atomic energy?

Kapitza: I think it is of the most vital importance to cultural development all over the world.

Bland: How could atomic energy help the Soviet Union, for example, in its work of reconstruction?

Kapitza: In the same way as in any other country, which tries to progress in the development of its culture.

Bland: Now, Professor Kapitza, in the United States recently, as you know, scientists have abandoned their traditional neutrality on political issues, and have been rather remarkably outspoken on matters of legislation affecting atomic energy. Mr. Corwin would like to know whether you believe that the scientist's responsibilities as a citizen are equal to those he has as a technician.

Kapitza: I think the scientist has *more* responsibility than any other citizen.

Bland: Then you feel that scientists are perfectly right in speaking up and airing their views on the matter of the use of atomic energy?

Kapitza: Certainly, because scientists see much better than anybody else, all the possible uses of atomic energy.

Bland: How do you feel about the use of atomic energy as a weapon?

Kapitza: It is the same as using electricity for the electric chair. (laughs)

Bland (laughing): But do you approve of it?

Kapitza: As you approve of electrocution in an electric chair.

Bland: In other words, you don't approve?

Kapitza (laughing): I think not.

Bland: May I ask on what particular field of work or research you are presently engaged?

Kapitza: My usual research: first, in the area of extreme low temperatures, secondly, with liquid helium, and the great phenomena occurring in intense magnetic fields.

Bland: Mr. Corwin asks what branches of science, outside of atomic sciences, you see as assuming the greatest importance in the next 20 to 50 years?

Kapitza: Well, that is difficult to answer—but I think the most important are the social sciences, those which could improve social conditions throughout the world, and which are fully neglected at the present time.

Bland: Lastly, Professor Kapitza, what message, if any, do you have for scientists of the world?

Kapitza: Peace and collaboration.

Bland: And for the peoples of the world?

Kapitza: Exactly the same. Peace and collaboration.

While Bland was having the fun and privilege of these interviews, I was stewing my way through my strep throat, and in a few days I got back into action with a retake of my meeting with Moscow's Radio Committee; this time Nick arranged for Vasili Anamatsky, Chief Editor of Literary Broadcasting, to attend. He was blond, and looked like a twin brother of Frank Stanton, president of CBS. Same complexion, same build, and, as it developed, same sense of humor.

> **NC:** Now Mr. Anamatsky, could you tell us something about the tastes of Soviet audiences in literature and drama, as you have found them in practice on the air?
>
> **Anamatsky:** First of all the listeners like good broadcasts. It would be difficult to answer in greater detail. It would amount to reading or delivering a long paper on the subject. But still I would like to say that they want high quality.
>
> **NC:** How do they indicate that they want high quality, by letters?
>
> **Anamatsky:** Oh yes, we get a great many letters, particularly after a bad broadcast. They make sad reading.
>
> **NC:** How long does it take them to forgive you?
>
> **Anamatsky (laughing):** Our listeners are probably the same as they are in other countries: very quick to forgive because they no sooner get annoyed with one broadcast than they have five other broadcasts to listen to.
>
> **NC:** Well now, I take it that the Soviet listener wants to hear the classics, wants to hear your great writers and playwrights— Pushkin, Tolstoi, Chekov.
>
> **Anamatsky:** The listener gets lots of opportunity to hear the classics, as more than half of our broadcasts are devoted to the best Russian writers of all kinds. For example, in a recent series of broadcasts, in connection with the tenth anniversary of Gorki's death, no less than 85 readings were given.
>
> **NC:** When you say readings, do you mean just straightaway readings, or are these dramatizations of the work?
>
> **Anamatsky:** Both. For instance, among these broadcasts was a production of a play by Gorki, which was never staged anywhere. It was an unfinished work by Gorki, and it was made into a radio production.
>
> **NC:** Do you have anything like serials here—continued stories from day to day or week to week?

Anamatsky: Only readings.

NC: Could you tell me about tastes musical and otherwise?

Anamatsky: Listeners are very fond of Russian music. Both classical and folk music.

NC: What about American jazz?

Anamatsky: Of course, it is good fun listening to American jazz, but you can't dance all the time. It becomes a bore.

NC: Is there any particular interest in American writing, or in works originally written in English?

Anamatsky: The most interesting and best works of American literature are translated, and people read them with quite a lot of interest.

NC: No, I don't mean reading them, I mean hearing them on the radio.

Anamatsky: I didn't finish. After all, we don't get such enormous quantities of literature from abroad. We broadcast translations of American fiction and American literature— those which have the greatest artistic merit, for example, [Erskine] Caldwell's book of his own boyhood. And then there was another broadcast—but I can't recall the name of the author because I didn't like the book.

NC: I see. You were looking straight at me when you said that.

Anamatsky: No, on the contrary. My colleagues and I are not making our first acquaintance with you today. We have known of you for some time, beginning with a translation of your book *Thirteen by Corwin.* Thirteen is an unlucky number—but the plays were mostly good, and we are very glad to see you here now—not in the book, but in the flesh.

NC: Now that you have taken care of my ego, I will go beyond to ask whether there is any hope of ever producing this writer, Corwin, on the Soviet air?

Anamatsky: Every playwright should hope that his plays will be produced all over the world. Otherwise he would be a poor playwright.

NC: That's dodging the question.

Anamatsky: I haven't seen Corwin offering me a play to be produced in Russia.

NC: Corwin hereby offers all his plays to be produced . . . and, in turn, I would like to take back with me a Russian radio script to be produced in America.

Anamatsky: I will be very pleased to make the exchange.

NC: Now, considering this microphone as an instrument which will enable you to speak, as I am speaking to you now, to many American listeners, what would you like to say to Americans about radio, about peace, about the future?

Anamatsky: About the weather. (Laughs). Let me say that I believe the weather shouldn't be upset by all sorts of artificially manufactured storms.

NC: Well, that charity can begin right at home because it has been storming here every day this week. Do you mean "weather of the world unite"?

Anamatsky: I mean weather of the world: CLEAR! As for radio, the greatest possible invention would be if it were possible to invent a microphone that would not allow a lie to pass. That would make ether a very good medium. You mentioned in one of your plays, Mr. Corwin, about a character whose head had no other function than to keep his ears apart. Unfortunately, there are too many people working in radio whose heads perform no other function. And everyone who likes radio and works for radio, should try to get these people out of the business, and to have nothing but truth on the air. As to the future, I will repeat what I understand Professor Kapitza told you the other day—"peace and collaboration."

NC: That is a very clear statement and I would like to know if all people working for the Soviet radio feel as you do.

Anamatsky: I don't think anybody here will say anything different.

NC: Well, now seriously, that is a fine statement, and it will be a privilege to convey it to America.

Anamatsky: I don't know whether Americans will consider it a privilege to hear it.

NC: You underestimate Americans.

Anamatsky: No, I simply don't overrate myself.

A few nights after my exchange with Mr. Anamatsky I was privileged to be the subject of a formal critique. The Russians go in strong for literary criticism of each other's work, and only once before, in the case of John Hersey's visit to Moscow a year earlier, had they opened their forum to a foreigner. They then dissected his novel *A Bell for Adano*. Early in my visit, Voks had hurriedly translated my *On a Note of Triumph* into Russian, and had distributed copies to 15 critics, all of whom read it and came armed to the meeting at Voks headquarters.

Seated around a long oak table were Mr. and Mrs. Karaganov, Schneerson, and 13 others, most of whose names, I regret to confess, mean little to me, but included a Shakespearian actor, the director of the State Moscow Jewish Theater, and the director of the Soviet Literary and Music Agency. Using the same clinical procedure for me as for their own writers, each critic took a turn commenting on my script (sometimes commenting on each other's comments), and I was given unlimited time, as last speaker, to make rebuttal.

A representative criticism, by Victor Shklovsky, who had lost a son in the war, was that in recounting the Allied victory over the Nazis, I had not given the Soviet Union due credit. Shklovsky was bald, in his 60's, and looked like a mild version of composer Jean Sibelius. He spoke movingly, with tears in his eyes, about the loss of sons, brothers, fathers, by so terribly many Russian families. Then, (in part), on apportioning credit:

> We Soviet people don't claim to—don't expect to be—don't want to be praised all the time, lauded to the skies for what we've done. But historical justice demands—and our duty to

those who are buried, demands—not to forget facts learned from the war, and the proportion of these facts: not to forget the difference between Stalingrad and Tobruk.

Another critic, whose name is lost to my notebook but whose voice is preserved in Bland's recording, felt that in answer to the question "Whom have we beaten?" I badly failed to identify the sponsor of fascism:

This fascist whom we've beaten, this killer of nations, where did he come from? He wasn't born spontaneously, for there must have been poisonous institutions that nourished him. The answer is simple; we say fascism was nourished by the capitalist world, the world, which in its imperialistic phase revealed its nature, its man-eating nature.

The rebuttal which I made at the very end seemed well received by so critical a group—and there was much laughter at some of my best points. And at the end, spontaneous applause.

One evening we went to see a circus from Azerbaijan. It was thoroughly enjoyable and had more color, dash, and comedy than I have found in any American circus. The theater, circular like a bullpen, was small. The entire performance, three acts long, took place in a circular area covered most of the time by a hand-woven rug. The exotic color and the people, the music and the language, gave me a great exhilaration that comes from new and completely strange surroundings.

We were up early the next morning and off to the sports parade at Dynamo Stadium. We were quite a while getting in, and Bland was extremely surly because of the limitation of space in which we had to operate. It was a hot day, bordering on too hot, and we arrived more than an hour early.

The entrance requirements were complex indeed, Nick having to do a great deal of legwork and we having to show our passports half a dozen times. Stalin was there, though we did not get to see him. The multitude did, however, and the ovation from the 80,000 was something worth preserving on our recorder.

The parade itself and various events which followed it, though too long (six hours, almost), were the most spectacular and colorful demonstration that I have ever seen. At times I was completely stopped by the sheer inadequacy to convey the tempo, drive, and precision of the spectacle. To me there was above all an enormous zest and pride in the performance, and the sight of that many bronzed, healthy bodies was gladdening and rewarding. Gymnastics, choreography, brilliant unison of choral effects, the singing, the well-modulated music on the loudspeakers, the hailing of Stalin, the management of props and settings, all was done with magical speed and efficiency.

We were some time getting out of the stadium area, even though we left before the program was finished. For a while it looked as though we might have to wait until Stalin himself had departed, for he was sticking to the finish of a regulation football match. But Nick talked his way through excessive red tape and we squeezed our car through. At an early point we were detoured, and the route took us through some of the cruelest slums I have ever seen.

Back at the hotel, I packed—a long job after our two-week spreading out. Awakened at 5:00 a.m., it was a completely lovely morning and I enjoyed the long drive—40 km—to the airport. There we were early, but absorbed our time in jest, picture taking, coffee drinking, and general clearance of passport and customs. Then at 8:10, ten minutes after we were scheduled to take off, we were away to the west backtracking our route to Warsaw in a great diversion that carried us all the way back to Paris before we could make our connections for Rome.

6

Land of Coalition
Czechoslovakia

I interviewed a dozen miners — men + women.

From Moscow to Prague is a distance of about 1,200 miles, as a plane flies. It was an unsettled day in which the weather changed from country to country. The land beneath us, with its frequent streams, rivers, and lakes, looked as green and innocent as though it had never heard the names of old wars, nor the rumors of new ones. Yet, not long ago, over every inch of the distance we were consuming so quickly and comfortably, armies had fought, blood had been mixed in streams and rivers; villages had been sacked; cities bombed. A dead man for every foot of the way.

We flew through a huge and handsome cloud formation and landed at Prague at 3:00—a half hour ahead of schedule. There we sailed through customs. The press was on hand—including the first movie camera staff I've seen so far. There was a great stack of mail waiting for me, and after a bit of sightseeing on the drive in, I dived into it.

Prague is a graceful city, baroque and Gothic, with a skyline of radio transmitters and cathedral spires, its ancient history is obscure; but Czechoslovakia's modern history, the whole world knows only too well. This country, slightly smaller than Wisconsin, was the republic handed over to Hitler at Munich, by agreement of two sister democracies. It was the vortex down which all of Europe would be drawn.

I was naturally anxious to see what betrayal and occupation and the trials of reconstruction had done to Czechoslovakia; whether its people were happy and confident; whether they were friendly to the United States; how they felt about Russia; whether they were, as we'd been told along the way, a bridge between East and West; whether they were in a mood to embrace the concept of One World.

It seemed that almost everybody we met in Prague had either personally suffered or was related to someone who had been tortured or killed by the Nazis. Young Jan Silvera, for example, who assisted us with our recordings, was the only one in a family of 18—including parents, brothers, sisters, and uncles—who was not executed by the Nazis. Our interpreter, Mrs. Slavka Gergorava, escaped from the country in order to aid the Czech resistance in London, and she was pursued by the Gestapo under circumstances resembling a spy melodrama.

Yet, none of these people seemed bitter or cynical. They were resolved to do everything they could not to let it happen again, but their resolution was never vindictive; it was calm, reasoning, and vigilant.

My interview with President Eduard Benes was at the Hradchany Palace. It was the first time the president made a recording and he did this in spite of no prior warning the interview would be committed to the wire. Lee and I had been kept waiting for an hour, but I felt it was within presidential prerogatives. I found Mr. Benes the most friendly and animated statesman I have yet interviewed.

I asked him whether it was true that Czechoslovakia had been the quickest to regain solid footing after the war, and if so, why. He replied:

> It is true. The reasons are complicated and numerous. I can tell you only a few of them. First, we had not been devastated in the

war in such a degree as many of the European countries were. Second, the German occupation had a special result on the morale of the Czech population: we never resigned, never; our morale was very high at the moment when the Germans began to be beaten, and so when the work of reconstruction began in our country, we were psychologically and morally better equipped than other countries. The third reason was that we felt that we had in no way contributed to the general disaster of the world and of Czechoslovakia. The war began with Munich.

He described the attitude and condition of his country one short year after liberation:

> Every Czech must be anti-fascist, and every Czech must be against any revival of fascism everywhere. Because fascism is connected intimately with the greatest injustice that has been made against us. . . . You can see in the streets of Prague everybody's working, everybody is enthusiastic. There is a great élan, a very great enthusiastic spirit for the work, and all know that they are working for a new liberty and a new independence.

That afternoon we drove out to Kladno, the mining city northwest of Prague, and went down into the Benes pits recently nationalized and named after the president. In no time, I was surrounded by miners, each eager to speak into the microphone, to be heard above the din of the machinery. My first question was whether they were worried about another war:

> **Miner:** We are afraid of war mainly because there is still Germany, which has so many Nazis and fascists who are allowed to carry on as before, and also, another reason is there is the Franco Spain, which is always a new incentive for another war. . . . We feel secure in our free liberated republic, but as soon as we look abroad, we can't have that feeling of security.

I asked the group whether it was more inclined to the East or West, and I got an answer that was a fair indication of how deeply Munich affected their attitudes, and how well they remember it:

Miner: With 99 percent we incline toward the East and only 1 percent we incline toward the West. We are Slavs and we belong to the large Slavonic group of nations, and whenever we look at the past, we know what has happened to us from the West.

Another miner responded: "I would like to say that we are inclined toward the East for the simple reason because it was the Red Army that liberated us."

It was clear that their orientation was toward the Soviet Union. They spoke of their "Soviet brothers." Some in the group were highly voluble on foreign affairs. They seemed to hold me personally responsible for the disposition of Trieste, the American policy toward Spain, and our occupation policy in Germany. They were critical of some of America's internal race relations; some exhorted me to nationalize American coal mines.

I asked one of the workers what, if he could make a wish tonight that might come true tomorrow, he would wish for:

Well I wish this, that all the gentlemen from the West and from the East would realize that we are men, that we are human beings, and that they would adjust their politics according to that; that they would adjust their politics to serve humanity, to serve mankind, as long as they don't do this, we won't have any peace.

When we were through recording and ready to leave, a delegation came over and asked, in a tone of self-reproach, whether perhaps they had not been too outspokenly critical of America, hence unfriendly to me as a visitor. I assured them I had wanted them to speak their minds, and not say things merely to please me.

We were to have interviewed some of the women who survived the Nazi massacre in the nearby village of Lidice, but our timing wasn't coordinated, so we headed home. I was a full hour late, sweaty and dirty from the mine. But I washed hastily and then joined a small dinner party of diplomats. There were card tricks, stories, and yarns about U.S. Intelligence during the war.

The following afternoon in Prague, we drank coffee with and talked to some students who were planning a World Congress for the following month. These young citizens of the world, too, were insistent on the anti-fascist character of their movement. I found that in Czechoslovakia, and in most of the Europe conquered and occupied by Hitler, the terms of "fascist" and "fascism" took on a different meaning from what was generally given them back home.

In America, to a great many people, "fascist" is merely a bad name you call a person whose politics you don't like; it's a term thrown about loosely when a group breaks in to a heated argument. Some of us are prone to call each other fascists or communists over issues ranging from labor unions through rent control to atomic energy.

But in a country like Czechoslovakia, a fascist means something quite real, not theoretical. The people of Prague saw fascism march down their main street; they saw their friends taken out of their homes and shot; they were tortured.

Dr. Cebe, for example—a soft-spoken lawyer in his early 40's, a father of three children, was active in the Czech underground, and was caught. He told of the refined tortures of the Gestapo, such as putting a 100-watt electric bulb close to his face for eight hours on end. For a year he was chained, night and day, in solitary confinement. He was finally sentenced to death. I asked him whether at any time he had lost hope:

> Well, sometimes—to be quite sincere—sometimes I had no hope because several times the priest came in my cell and told me "Prepare yourself, you will be hung—you'll be guillotined." Naturally, only one hour later he came back and said, "It has been postponed. You must hope." And—well. But friends from other cells, twice or three times a week, they came out and they were guillotined.

I asked Dr. Cebe what he, as a man to whom fascism and war held a deep personal meaning, would most urgently recommend to the United Nations:

This is what would be my humble message to the United Nations:
Not to breed the idea that there is a necessity of a war between
the East and West—between Eastern and Western conceptions
of life. I know that this is the last hope of fascism.

One day Bill Kugeman of the American Embassy drove us out
to the town of Dobris, to visit a palace occupied by an association
of Czech writers. The drive began in the heart of Prague, which
is a city as noisy as it is beautiful. Prague, after Warsaw and Moscow, had an air of prosperity. Stocks seemed to be high in stores,
produce was plentiful. You could even buy canned tomato juice—
a luxury unheard of in most of the world outside of the United
States—for the equivalent of six cents, without any ration tickets.

We drove through the busy, narrow streets, past a monument
enshrining the first Russian tank to enter the city in the battle
for liberation, then into the outskirts, following the bank of the
Vltava to the countryside—to the romantic, nonpolitical Bohemia
of song and legend. We went through magnificent pine groves,
and wound among high, wooded hills. We were reminded, looking out at all this first-class scenery, of how much first-class culture, how much good literature and music had come out of this
little country.

Czechoslovakia is understandably proud of its artists, and it
seems generally to take loving care of its culture—at least if treatment of writers is any indication. When we reached the palace
at Dobris, we found it to be pretty much the kind you have built
for yourself at sometime or other in an architectural daydream—
big, sprawling, opulent, with formal gardens, a swimming pool, a
library, a ballroom, marble bathtubs, and all that.

The new coalition government decided its writers were a
national asset, and so it bought and turned over to a Writers'
Syndicate this expensive palace. To join the syndicate, a writer
must have three published books to his credit, or three plays produced. Then a writer may, if he chooses, live at the palace for a
stated period of the year, meals included, with or without family,
for two dollars a day.

When we arrived, children were running around chasing puppies. I asked their parents whether they had come there to work or rest. The interpreter responded:

When they came here, they called it a House of Recreation, but they hope it will develop into a House of Creation, and now it seems that people really are beginning to work here. When you awaken in the morning, you can hear about ten typewriters rattling away. So, it looks as though something is going to be created here.

For a whole afternoon I talked with a score of poets, novelists, essayists, and playwrights, and it was pretty clear that they had a highly socialized sense of art. A young woman novelist, Miss Stenglova, for instance, had a personal formula for the relationship of the individual to the state: "I am a Czech, and whatever happens to my nation happens first to me, so that all I can do with my work is to say, 'I am a good Czech.'"

After a splendidly produced luncheon and our good conversations with the writers, I peeled my coat off and went around the superlative grounds, absorbing as much sunlight as I could.

Back in Prague, it was a pleasant surprise for me to find an American flag made of flowers blooming handsomely at a monument to Woodrow Wilson on one of the main streets. I mentioned this in the course of an interview with Jan Papanek, a Czech Minister Plenipotentiary. "Czechs appreciate and are thankful for all the help they received during the war from the United States," he said. "And this flag is only a small sign of what they feel, what they express and will be expressing in the future."

Mr. Papanek described the changes in the Czechoslovak economy brought about by the coalition government—a government consisting of four parties: Social Democrat, National Socialist (not in the Hitler meaning of National Socialist, by the way), People's Catholic, and Communist—with the latter holding a plurality in the number of seats. He remarked that these changes, such as the nationalization of heavy industries, while retaining free enterprise in most of the lesser categories, were for the good of the country, and though at variance with American practice, need not alienate the friendship of Americans: "We hope that America will understand us. We are trying to reshape our national, our economic life. We are trying to do it for the best of our people, all of them, and we are set to succeed."

Not the least remarkable grain of hope for One World was the example of the scientific body that I found working in Czechoslovakia. This was the Medical Teaching Mission of the Unitarian Service Committee, a group of American doctors who had volunteered to bring to the Czech people some of the medical and surgical techniques and drugs from which they had been cut off during the long Nazi occupation. These doctors, working without compensation and taking time away from their extensive practices at home, lectured to the medical faculties of Czech universities, performed operations, and conducted clinics. This gesture of goodwill, which had the full cooperation of our State Department, was not lost on the Czechs. One of several appreciative articles to appear in the Czech press was headlined, "This is What International Relations Ought to Be."

We also visited the home of the famed professor of philosophy, Jan Kozak, who, at the time of the Nazi invasion in 1939, had two hours to pack his belongings and flee his country. During the war, he found refuge at Oberlin College in Ohio. He criticized both America and Russia:

> In the United States, too much of equality has been sacrificed to liberties. In the Soviet Union maybe too many liberties have been sacrificed to the ideal of equality. For the time being we must place the emphasis on freedom from want, and freedom from fear. You will understand us; but we are determined to implement all Four Freedoms, and we shall do it in this country, take my word for that.

The professor said he had some questions about what he had observed of world affairs since he had last been in the United States:

> President Roosevelt, whom I loved very much, once said the only thing we must fear is fear. How many of you Americans have

fear? Do you still believe that free enterprise—I mean without any governmental interference—can prevent or solve economic depressions? Are you sure that you are going to have no more economic depression?

Of the economy in Czechoslovakia, Professor Kozak was more certain. He said that in carrying out the nationalization of heavy industries the coalition government had performed a practically painless operation, because it meant cutting those industries loose from the tentacles of *German* financial control, and did not, therefore, dislocate Czech interests. He credited the coalition government with having brought the Czech very far, very quickly.

This from the country that, such a short time ago, was dismembered at Munich, and later invaded by the invincible Wehrmacht. This from little Czechoslovakia, which was to have been an obedient province of Greater Germany for the next thousand years—the thousand years of the Fascist Millennium.

Nine years ago, Czechoslovakia stood at the crossroads of war. Today, perhaps, it stands in the position of a bridge at the crossroads of peace. To many of her people, the way to the future is the middle way, the way they are traveling—a way that reconciles socialism and private enterprise by running them side-by-side. From where they're standing, looking toward horizons ringed by Russians, Germans, Poles, Rumanians, and Hungarians, with a monument to the Red Army on one street and an American flag in flowers, on another, they believe this way of theirs is a short-cut to the Grand Concourse called One World.

On our last morning in Prague, a crisis almost developed over my shoes. The hall porter had kept them four days and it took me 45 minutes to get them back before Kugeman drove us to the airport through a delightful morning. There we boarded a comfy 21-passenger aircraft. Andre Simone the Czech correspondent and author of *J'accuse: The Men Who Betrayed France* introduced himself. We had a long talk as we flew over beautiful country.

❧

7

Friends, Romans, Egyptians
Italy and Egypt

By God, I piloted a plane for 18 minutes today!

From Prague we flew to Rome, doglegging via Paris and Marseilles. We found Italy in great turmoil following its recent elections. Hunger and unemployment were on the upswing. We took our equipment in an Army car down to a street corner where Black Market cigarette salesmen ply their trade and recorded interviews with Roman citizens. They were plenty noisy and crowded me until I could barely breathe.

Not far from this corner, in another time of hunger and unemployment, Benito Mussolini offered a way out. He stood on the balcony of the Palazzo Venezia and led the people to believe that war was glorious, and that democracy was a flop, that if they just handed over their liberties and kept their mouths shut, they would all be rich and well fed and happy. He led them to war for fascism against Ethiopians and Spanish Loyalists, against a collapsing France, and, finally, against us and our allies.

Now, their Duce, their empire, and a good many of their relatives and friends were dead. A lot of their country was smashed up, their jobs were thinned out, and their food was low. They had turned in desperation to fascism a generation ago, and now, after disaster heaped upon disaster, they were back in desperation. We heard complaints from bewildered people who felt that

Italy had been betrayed; that America, England and Russia had broken promises.

Just as Nazism did not end in Germany with the suicide of its bigwigs and the surrender or its armies, neither did 30 years of fascist education disappear in Italy when Mussolini was strung up by the heels. The impress of fascism is still on the minds of those who suffered under it. "If you don't treat us well today," one man said through the interpreter, "we'll make the war tomorrow."

The depression, confusion and desperation reflected in this random group of Romans was a fair cross-section of what was going on all over Italy. In the same week of the interviews, a mob attempted to lynch the prefect of Milan; there was a political strike in Como; fist fights broke out in the newly elected Constitutional Assembly in Rome; the treasury reported that the national deficit would total 150 percent of national income; hundreds of fascists granted amnesty by the new government were bragging openly that they had always been fascists and were proud of it; a mob in Gorizia jeered Allied officers in the street; the Italian General Confederation of Labor ordered a one-hour work stoppage as a symbol of Italy's attitude toward the Paris Peace Conference; unemployment figures passed the two-million mark; there was a national strike of hotel workers, another of petroleum work-ers, and a threatened strike of street-car workers; right-wingers declared that they were fearful that the country's troubles would turn her toward Russia; left-wingers charged the government with attempting to turn the country against Russia; from the provinces came editorials accusing the Allies of forgetting Italy's sacrifices to help defeat Germany; from Naples came reports of a new wave of highway banditry.

Almost all of these incidents and disturbances were reflected in what these people said spontaneously. Again and again, Italians shouldered their way through the crowd to reach the microphone, if only to speak a few words, such as, "My mother is American and I am Italian. We are in Italy, in very bad condition."

There were so many trying to be heard, pushing their way to the meager platform of the mike I held in my hand, that I had trouble keeping them from all speaking at once, and had to beg them several times to take turns. "We want work, give us work! We can't go on like this!" Two things kept coming through insistently: first, that the people were poor and hungry and wanted work; second, that there were many similarities between the situation they were in today and the situation Italy was in back when they were led into fascism in 1920.

As foreigners, we had, of course, attracted a crowd with our microphone; but otherwise the streets of Rome were fairly quiet— in spite of the latent turbulence of the people, which only a few weeks later would erupt into fatal rioting. It was still early August; the sun was very hot; Romans who could afford to ride on noisy little post-war buses (really only motorcycles with a sort of trailer attachment) headed for the beaches some 20 miles away.

For most of the Allied-occupation officers and the better-off Italians, living wasn't bad at all—good food; golf; swimming; the country club out toward the airport that Count Ciano had built for his blackshirt cronies; the parks, museums; the fine music. Stores were full of wonderful goods from all over, if you had the price. The city's classic remains, the shrines of tourism, the grandeur that was Rome were still untouched.

I went to see *Aida* at the ancient ruins of the Baths of Caracalla. Having never seen the opera, I was even more impressed. I was bowled over by the magnitude of the amphitheatre, the size and splendor of the production. The night was perfect—warm, clear. You could almost forget that in the 70 years since Verdi's great opera was first produced, Italy had very little to sing about, what with a dozen major and minor depressions and seven wars—two of them world wars. But I mused upon the pyramid of ruin symbolized before me; the ruin of the Egyptian civilization depicted in the play; the ruins of Rome, tangible before us; the ruin of modern Italy—heaped layer upon layer.

We interviewed spokesmen for three of the political parties: Action, Christian Democrat, and Communist. I requested, but did not get to see, a spokesman for the Socialists. Ugo La Malfa, of the Action Party, a young, dark, intense man, received us in his apartment six flights up from a narrow street in the center of the city. His party had been badly beaten in recent elections and was now represented by only seven seats. Malfa was quick to acknowledge the seriousness of Italy's condition. He said there was a peril of fascist resurgence in all of Europe if economic difficulties were not solved. However, he differed from most other Italians we interviewed, in believing that the rebuilding of a strong Germany—including its full economic potential—was essential to Europe's well-being and safety.

The next interview was with the Communist leader, Palmiro Tagliatti, a short, plain man, in his office overlooking the busy Via Nationale. He was at home with extemporaneous speech. He said that in order to implement recovery, "Italy might well take an example from the conduct of internal affairs in the United States under President Roosevelt." He said he didn't mean a program of socialism, but one in which the government, by aiding and working together with private industry, could come toward the needs of the people. He gave an example of what he meant:

> Italy at the moment is home to hundreds of thousands of men, women, and children, who live without houses, in fact, who live in caverns. If you visit the beach of Ostia, you will find bathing houses built there made of cement. Now it is noteworthy that in Italy itself, this same cement is not used to build the houses for which these hundreds of thousands of people have such urgent need. The program of the Italian government, therefore, which in the first stages has procured this cement from America, should be to assure that this cement which is brought from such a distance, is used for the benefit and good of the common people, rather than for the exclusive benefit of a privileged few.

The Italian Prime Minister, Alcide De Gasperi, leader of the Christian Democratic Party, which has upwards of 200 seats in the Government, was our next interviewee. We were received by Mr. De Gasperi in his large office in the Vimanale Palace. Unlike the other party spokesmen, he spoke in generalities, of "the common tragedy of fascism uniting all men of all creeds together." The prime minister charged that the press had all too often become an instrument of misunderstanding by magnifying evils and failing to report what he called "incidents of goodwill." His only comment on the situation within Italy referred to dissatisfaction over the clauses of the Paris treaty as "a love delusion," and hoped that friendship between the Allies and Italy would not be for long impaired.

My request for audience with Pope Pius XII had been relayed through the office of Myron C. Taylor, President Truman's personal representative to the Vatican, and the appointment was quickly made. However, the possibility of recording the interview was quickly nixed when the papal secretary learned we had already recorded various presidents, Prime Minister Atlee, and, in Rome, Premier De Gasperi and Palmiro Tagliatti. The secretary was aghast: "You are not looking for One World if you see people like Tagliatti. It would be irreverent to record Tagliatti and His Holiness on the same machine." That took care of the recording, but we were made to understand that I could ask His Holiness whatever questions I had in mind, providing the questions were written out and submitted in advance.

Protocol dictated that if the Pope in the course of our meeting, wished to reply to the questions, he would bring them up himself; if not, I was not to propose them. I wrote out four questions and submitted them. The audience had been granted for myself and two associates, which meant Bland and interpreter John Mecklin, who was the CBS Rome correspondent and writer for the *Roman Daily American*. Hilda Wane, a secretary and assistant who had accompanied us wherever we had gone in Rome, and had been present at every interview, was unhappy not to have been included, but the formal, printed invitation to the Papal apartments, specified only three men. We went by car to the Vatican, and parked below the palace, and left Hilda to mind the recording machine.

We entered the building, into which hundreds of children dressed for confirmation were streaming, ascended in one of a bank of spacious elevators to a floor on which were situated reception halls and a succession of small rooms depending from a stately corridor. The children, together with attending priests, were gathered in the largest of these rooms. On presenting our credentials we were led through six rooms in which various smaller groups were waiting to see the Pope, through a seventh room in which five people were assembled, and into an eighth, which was empty. Here we were directed to sit on an upholstered bench until His Holiness appeared; then our guide, a tall man in a scarlet robe, left us.

The room, about the size of an ample pantry, was richly appointed, its walls covered by a patterned fabric. Overhead was a simple electric light fixture, its bulb burning. After ten minutes, the guide returned, motioned for us to stand, and directed us to line up before the room's only window. At this moment an electric bell rang somewhere down the corridor, and the overhead light went out, leaving only subdued daylight coming through a silken white curtain over the window. The Pope entered, smiling, wearing a white robe and white skull cap. He moved quickly toward us, extending his hand; he greeted me first, then Mecklin and Bland, pronouncing our names as he did. He spoke at once of the heat of the city, then of the recent canonization of Mother Cabrini, the first American to be admitted to sainthood. In good English with a moderate accent, he said he was sorry we had missed the ceremonies in the Vatican.

This Pope, Engenio Pacelli, had sat on the papal throne through the most desperate years in the history of the world; the Italy around his enclave had suffered and bled; bombs had fallen within sight of Michelangelo's soaring dome. The Pope seemed older, smaller, milder than I had imagined him from his pictures.

What part of the United States was I from, he asked. When I replied Boston, he remarked that he had been there, liked the city, had friends in it. Then he asked about the Willkie mission, where I had been, where I was going. Willkie's concept of One World, he said, was an early Christian concept; the Church embraced it now as always.

The Pope in this way tactfully answered one of the four questions I had submitted; the other three, more specific and temporal, he did not touch upon. Now he passed to a blessing of the Willkie mission, and then to personal blessings. Were any of us Catholics? None of us was, but I said that my brother (Alfred) had married a Catholic girl. Would I like to carry a rosary blessed by himself, to my sister-in-law? I said I would feel privileged to do so. Would Bland and Mecklin like to take home rosaries for their Catholic friends? They would indeed. His Holiness sent for three rosaries, and in the time it took for them to be delivered, we discussed the forthcoming itinerary of our trip, and the use that was to be made of material gathered on the way. Then the rosaries came, in little paper enclosures; the Pope blessed them and us, we shook hands, and the audience was over.

When we returned to Hilda, waiting in the car in the courtyard of the palace, I saw at a glance that she was consumed with curiosity, and as we approached I whispered to Mecklin and Bland to fall in with some impromptu reportage, a concoction expressly for her amazement.

"How was it?" she asked, eagerly.

"Wonderful," said Bland.

"Tell me everything! What kind of room did he meet you in?"

"This may surprise you," I answered, "but he received us in his den."

"Den?"

"Yes," Mecklin concurred, "it was terribly informal."

"How was he dressed?" Hilda pressed.

"Sports jacket."

Hilda's mouth opened in astonishment. "You mean that informal?"

"No tie. Shirt open at the collar."

"Are you kidding me?"

All three of us shook our heads solemnly, with an air of being amazed ourselves by the strangeness and unexpectedness of it.

"What did you discuss?"

"Oh, a number of things.—He offered us sandwiches."

"Good heavens! What kind?"

"Ham. He also offered us cigarettes."

"Oh come now," Hilda scoffed. "Don't try to tell me the Pope smokes cigarettes."

"No he doesn't. He smokes a pipe. He lit up while we were talking."

Hilda looked at me askance, not daring to believe me, yet not ruling out any possibility in a world as mad as this.

"I suppose he served you drinks," she said archly.

All three of us confirmed this with such instant and earnest unanimity that Hilda trembled on the edge of credulity.

"You mean he offered you hard liquor?"

"Yes."

"What was the drink?" she asked, now genuinely amazed.

I could not resist. "Vat Sistine Nine," I said.

That did it.

One day we climbed into a jeep and drove over the Appian Way up into the Albani Mountains, to the shattered village of Lanuvio to see the conditions of a typical war-torn sector. The plight of the villagers was one of the saddest of the many tragic things we encountered on this trip. Typical was a hungry family of ten living in an abandoned wine cellar among casks, cobwebs, dust, and vermin with stray garlands of onions hanging from the ceiling and a horse taking up most of the floor space. Ground space really, for there was no floor.

As in Rome, the people were not at all hesitant about speaking. All except little Mario, age 15. He was shy and stood well back in the group of villagers who crowded about our jeep. He was shy because he only had one foot; the stump of the other being exposed because he had no shoes. We finally got him to talk. He said he'd lost his foot in the same shell explosion that killed six members of his family: "We were eleven, and six died. Father, mother, three sisters, and a brother."

The mayor of Lanuvio, twenty-nine-year-old Hercules Frezzi, won election by a margin of nine votes. When we met him, he had been working and he was shirtless, unshaven, sweating from the heat of the day, and covered with dust from the rubble of the street. "What is your political affiliation?" I asked. "Communist party." He said he had been a Communist for two years and had joined that party because he was a worker.

Again, as in Rome, the people in the village asked mainly for work—they asked for it even above food. One man with the arresting name of Spartacus Peace told us: "In Italy we still have dignity left. We ask the United Nations, whether they be the Allies, whether they be Americans or the English, or whatever else they be, that instead of just sending us charity, that they assist to get us work."

During my stay in Italy, I looked up the film writer Sergio Amidei—a pleasant, graying, good-looking man—whose movie *Open City*, the story of the resistance of the Italian partisans, had won awards in many countries, including the United States. I had missed seeing the film in the States, and he screened it for me in a projection room. Afterwards we had a long talk about the way the world looked from the standpoint of an anti-fascist Italian whose work was already a symbol of his country's cultural rebirth.

He was gloomy about the international situation and the possible impact of the death of FDR:

> I felt within myself a disturbance, almost a heart attack, when I heard of the death of President Roosevelt. Because I felt that when Roosevelt died, there died a man who understood the problems of peoples, and who understood these problems above the lesser problems of American politicians. I'm inclined to think that lacking this leadership and understanding there is a danger that Americans will forget their responsibilities in—if you will pardon the word—"a drunkenness of victory."

I told Roberto Rossolini, the director of *Open City*, that I thought his film one of the great of all time and urged him to go to Hollywood, where he had an offer from Metro [MGM film studio]. He said he was merely curious, but listened solemnly to my warnings. Joining us for a meal after the screening was the hero of the Italian anti-Nazi resistance fighters, Rodolfo Benvenuto Sonego. This man, who rose to be chief of the partisans through his valor and skill, had never heard of Wendell Willkie. Not much news or information got through to the partisans in their mountain hideouts. But the idea of One World got through on its own. Sonego told us: "That's what we used to say when we were lost in the mountains, in heavy snow and rain, with nobody to protect us but the stars. Everyone said 'Why isn't there one world, one flag under which we could all march and be united?'"

The day before we left Italy was stifling hot. Perfect for a trip to Lido di Ostia, the nearest beach to Rome, for a swim in the Mediterranean. I used the enlisted men's club. I was groggy the next morning, which was no help to me in the matter of hurriedly packing. But I got away in a powerful sweat only 10 minutes late. There was some trouble with TWA about baggage and payment in the line. The plane seemed to take an unconscionably long time taking off.

We flew over terribly rugged country between Rome and Naples, then over the instep of the boot—Gulf of Taranto—and then down the heel. In a very short time we picked up the first of the Greek Islands—hot and dry and mostly barren—and flew over the wide strait that divides Greece. In the dimming light of the day, I saw the Corinth Canal, with the ship sunk by the Germans blocking its entrance. We landed at Athens and had a wonderful meal on TWA—took off an hour later.

Filaments of the Nile, fanning out in its delta, glowed palely with reflected moonlight. Alexandria was off to the west of our course, and not visible. After a while the moon set, and we started down ourselves. It was past midnight when we landed. The heat of the desert lingered in the still air. We had heard reports of the officiousness of Egyptian customs, and were prepared to see our equipment dismantled and our luggage thoroughly searched for subversive Zionist literature, but instead we were whisked through without a lock being opened or a zipper unzipped. This was entirely the work of George Polk, CBS Middle East correspondent. He had alerted customs officials that I was coming to see King Farouk on highly confidential business, and this intelligence had spread so widely that airport personnel bowed to us all the way from the door of the airplane to the seven-passenger limousine Polk rented for the occasion.

Polk did things up right. He had reserved rooms for us at Mena House, a posh hotel on the outskirts of the city, and he had his chauffeur drive us through sleeping Cairo, across the Nile and over a broad highway that ended at the hotel. When I reached my room, a bottle of Scotch, another of whiskey, and a carton of cigarettes stood on the bureau—compliments of Polk.

It was 2:00 in the morning by now, and warm. I showered, got into pajamas, went to the windows which had been curtained against the heat, and threw back the drapes. It was a clear, crystalline desert night. The sky was heavily powdered by the Milky Way; the familiar constellations were all there but extra brilliant, and slightly off course from the accustomed bearings of a New Yorker. Suddenly, as my eyes adjusted to the darkness of the night, I became aware of a remarkable opacity in the heavens. There was a whole area in which stars were blotted out. Was this the Coal Sack? No, that's in the other hemisphere, near the Southern Cross. Then could it be some other nebula, one of those clouds of sidereal trash that litter space? No, this opacity seemed oddly angular. Indeed, triangular. And then it dawned on me that I was looking at the bulk of a Pyramid. Polk, with a nice sense of theater, had deliberately kept from us the fact that Mena house stood right across from the Pyramid of Cheops, and near the Sphinx. He wanted us to make the discovery for ourselves.

Later in my stay I visited the temples, tombs and pyramids at Gizeh. Other travelers have expanded upon their majesty. But I was shocked to find Cheops, greatest monument of all antiquity, overrun by chiseling, racketeering guides. Here by the paws of the Sphinx, I could find no evidence of national pride in glories upon which poets and statesmen, aye, and Caesar and Napoleon, had dilated. Not a sign, not a marker, not even a "Don't Make Off With Any Stones or Shards" cautioned against the souvenir hunters that Mark Twain and other voyagers had long complained about. Instead, illiterate feillahins in sacklike galibiyehs, short-changing customers, insisting on stopping to tell one's fortune by drawing a circle in the dirt of a temple floor, clamoring to sell phony antique coins, refusing to take another step until you paid still more piastres to be conducted into some recess, and gabbing about superfluous statistics of construction. But the living were honored no better than the dead, as we found out in recordings around the city. Polk, who covered all of the Middle East for CBS and sent live newscasts to the States from the Marconi studios of Egyptian State Radio, had been in Cairo long enough to have picked up some Arabic, but in the interests of accuracy and range, he engaged as interpreter Marcelle Hitschmann, a small, attractive Levantine woman of jet black hair and eyes. Marcelle had been married to a Czech, hence the Hitschmann; she was proficient in English, Arabic, French and two or three Slavic languages, and was of unfailing assistance to Polk, who came everywhere with us, and to Bland and myself.

Our first interview was on a street near the vicinity of the royal palace. We intercepted the first person to come along. He was a boy, better dressed than most on Cairo's streets. I asked how many were in his family:

Boy: I got father, I got mother, I got sister and grandfather— I got everything.

NC: All living in the same place?

Boy: Yes.

NC: How many rooms?

Boy: Two rooms.

He said he was a mechanic, that he earned 15 piastres a day, which was the equivalent of 60 cents.

NC: What sort of food do you eat?

Boy: I eat in the morning gruel, I eat hot and cold meat, something like that.

NC: Do you buy all this at 15 piastres a day?

Boy: I take 15 piastres every day, I smoke the cigarette by five piastres and keep ten in my home to get some new food for myself.

George Polk: Do you have to pay food and rent and everything out of 15 piastres a day? That's 60 cents a day that you make, and you pay for all your family? How many children do you have?

Boy: I have three children.

Polk: How old are you?

Boy: I'm about 16 years old.

He said he wasn't worried about anything; said he had heard a rumor that the war was over, but he wasn't sure, He was somewhat better informed about American jargon, for he suddenly used the phrase, "hubba, hubba."

NC: You've seen some American movies, eh?

Boy: Yeah.

NC: Is that where you got "hubba, hubba?"

Boy: No, some soldier, he walk in street, he make "Hubba, hubba, take it easy."

Through Mrs. Hitschmann we next questioned a man named Abda, who said he was a servant, earning seven Egyptian pounds a month, or about $21.

Polk: Are you happy with your life?

Abda: Well, who is happy?

NC: Why are you not happy?

Abda: Because everything is expensive.

I asked what he thought of Egypt's independence, of the situation in Palestine, and whether he knew the war was over.

Abda: I don't care about politics and about wars. Who cares about these things?

I asked whether he was at all interested in the world outside of Egypt; whether he would perhaps like to visit some other country.

Abda: Why should I go? If there is work somewhere else, all right, but I mean to go just like that? Where?

NC: Do you ever get to see a movie?

Abda: I never went to see one in my life.

NC: Would you like to go to see one?

Abda: Why should I go?

He said he had never read a book, that he never read newspapers, that he was not at all interested in these things. While this was going on, a crowd gathered, and there were hostile rumblings. When Polk started to ask questions of an Arab in a long blue tarboush, the Arab protested: "I don't like this idea, I think it is an insult to my dignity." Other people in the crowd said they were afraid of being recorded. I asked Marcelle what accounted for this attitude.

"Well, it is quite difficult to explain," she said. "First of all, it never happened to them before; and then, their technical knowledge is very small. And they do not know what this is; and just now especially they are not very friendly towards foreigners, and they are afraid of stating things definitely. They don't like people who ask them questions. They are always like that. You see, when people ask them questions, it generally brings trouble. It means there is a policeman who comes to ask them questions. Nobody ever asks what they think, unless there is a very definite purpose, and that's why they just dislike the idea, and they are afraid because it's all so strange for them."

As a respite from our recording one day, Polk, Bland and I went on a buggy ride through Cairo's bazaar. It was hot and dusty, and I was depressed by the pitiful condition of the people. I saw a leper; there were blind people, ragged people, shoeless and filthy urchins. A woman sat on a curbstone, suckling an infant; next to her, as casually as one might loll on a doorstoop, a child was defecating.

The new nationalism had taken hold, and Cairenes no longer felt obliged to pretend politeness to foreigners. One man, seeing a fez on Bland (he had bought one to send home and was wearing it idly) came up to him and sneered, "Now we are brothers, eh?" Another, holding a child in his arms, asked sardonically, "Want to buy a child? Polk showed us children of seven and eight, working in sidewalk foundries and auto repair shops—16 hours a day, for a few piastres. Everywhere there were diseased eyes—squinting, near-sighted, walleyed, blind.

Egypt was the eleventh country we had visited, and though we saw bad conditions elsewhere, this, for a traveler heading east, was the beginning of genuinely morbid ignorance, squalor and sickness. To the eye the city was attractive enough, both in its medieval and modern aspects; it was checkered with mosques and palaces, ancient walls, towers, domes; the old city had its bazaar and narrow, winding streets; the newer quarters, along the river, achieved a certain European colonial dignity. To the east, behind the citadel, stood barren hills, and beyond that, sandy desert. Just out of town was the edge of the western desert, and in between, the Nile, tree-shaded, romantic, polluted, supporting life and agriculture along its banks just as it had done since earliest history.

Egypt had been by turns Memphite, Theban, Syrian, Persian, Macedonian, Roman, Arabian, Turkish, French and British. Dozens of wars had swept up and down the Nile and had zigzagged across the deserts. And in all this time the only constant factor, static since the days of hieroglyphs, had been the oppression of millions, the poverty, the relentless ignorance. Before reaching Cairo I had seen enough to know that poverty is not the patent of any single country; that abject misery of millions was not peculiar to Egypt.

The crash of an economy in a distant land can make people poorer half a world away. Droughts, floods, wars, extravagances, inequities, all these have their bearing. But poverty occurs at its level worst, when combined with repression. And there was certainly that—oppression from the government, from the church of Islam, from the realities of life in Northeast Africa.

There were schools in Egypt for the better off; also health services, of a sort. But as we went around the city stopping people on the street, there was little to show the effect of either education or sanitation. In Medan Ismaili, one of the better sections of the city, I asked a cook named Achmed what he thought of conditions in the country. "Too many people no work," he replied, "too many people no eat, too many people no money." When I asked what he thought should be done, he answered that the government should open shops and factories in order to create more work. He said he was a Monarchist because he read in the papers that the King wanted to improve Egypt.

NC: Have you ever heard the word "fascism"?

Achmed: No.

NC: Have you ever heard the word "Nazi"?

Achmed: No.

NC: Have you ever heard of the word "Communist"?

Achmed: No.

NC: Have you ever heard of the word "Democracy"?

Achmed: Yes.

NC: What do you know about Democracy?

Achmed: It means everybody is the same.

The ignorance which lay like a pall over the people was not confined to any particular district. My recordings were made not in a backwoods area, but on the streets of the biggest city in Africa, a modernized, busy city that for centuries has had access to the best of Eastern and Western culture.

In the hope that samplings made thus far were not entirely representative of the man-in-the street, I tried again, still in another district. The first man here was a worker, father of two children, and sole support of his wife, mother, and father. He earned a dollar a day.

NC: Have you ever been outside of Cairo?

Worker: Never.

NC: Do you read?

Worker: I don't read. I don't write.

NC: Have you ever seen a moving picture?

Worker: No, no.

NC: Have you ever heard a radio?

Worker: I listen to music from the Egyptian State Broadcasting, but not to the news.

NC: On your own radio?

The question was not relayed by Marcelle who was interpreting. She explained to me that the only way people like him would hear radios would be to go to a cafe where one was in operation. We next talked to a man who said his home was four miles from the Nile. I asked when he had last seen the river. He said eight years ago.

A boy pushed his way to our microphone, and I questioned him:

NC: Have you ever gone to school?

Boy: I went only for two months to school, and then I left.

NC: How long ago was that?

Boy: About three years ego.

NC: I see. How old are you now?

Boy: Sixteen.

I said to Polk, "He looks about 13, doesn't he?" "Yes," he responded, "but generally they don't know their age." An airplane passed overhead a moment later, and I asked the boy whether he would like to fly in one. At first he said "No," and then he said, laughing, "Tomorrow, if I work for Hitler, maybe I will ride a plane."

NC: How did you hear about Hitler?

Boy: Well, during the war.

NC: Do you know Hitler is dead?

Boy: Nobody ever told me that Hitler is dead.

NC: Do you know who won the war?

Boy: Some people say the British, some people say Hitler.

NC: Have you ever thought you would like to find out, who really won the war? Are you curious to know?

It took some time to make the boy understand this last question; and in the process, a man of about 35 who was standing nearby, a cemetery caretaker, took part in the discussion. Finally they both answered it:

Boy: I don't care.

Caretaker: In the end Hitler will win.

The caretaker had an eye infection, and Polk told me that 90 percent of Egyptians were suffering from eye diseases, and that the incidence of blindness was very high. I asked the Arab what he was doing about his eye:

NC: Why don't you go to some clinic or something?

Caretaker: I have no money.

Polk: Aren't you afraid of going blind? So many persons are blind here. You see them wandering in the streets.

Caretaker: What should I do? God is there (points to the sky), and if God wants me to be blind, I'll be blind.

Marcelle explained to me, "The only thing they want is to be left alone; to die alone. When sick, they go to the magician and get a little piece of paper with a couple of cabalistic things written on it; or they buy a blue bead or a bit of turquoise or something like that, and they believe that maybe they will get better that way. Because of the Moslem faith, they always think that whatever happens, God wants it so. So if they die, they die because God wants it so. If the children die, God wants it so, and you cannot argue. You can't explain to them that there is God, but there are doctors too. They just don't believe in it."

One night Marcelle arranged a dinner party at her flat, which overlooked Cairo's famed Citadel, the Gawhara Mosque, and a series of lesser mosques. At the Citadel that evening there was to be a celebration of Egyptian independence. The Union Jack, which had flown over the Citadel for 65 years, was to come down, and the green flag of Egypt was to be raised by King Farouk.

Invited to the party, besides Bland and myself, were Polk, and NBC's Middle East correspondent John Donovan, who arrived in a jeep, ebullient and engaging. He insisted that before dinner, we all run over to the Macquattam Hills (the same from which limestone for the pyramids had been quarried) for a view of the city. We were almost at the base of these hills to start with, and in little time we were climbing a winding dirt road. But "dirt road" is an extravagant term: it was rutted, bumpy, stony, and powdery; we bounced, slid, groaned and heaved over that accursed road, raising clouds of fine dust and swallowing it by the cubic foot.

It turned out to be worth the trouble. When we reached the top, it was dusk; a three-quarter-plus moon had just risen. The sun, swollen and crimson, was going down in a blanket of haze, behind barred clouds stained deep purple. The ruins of an ancient mosque stood bare to the south, on the highest point of the hills; the Citadel, now far below, glowed like a jewel, its minarets electrically lit. The sun sank quickly, but a subdued shimmer lingered in the sky, and the whole of Cairo below took on a ghostly mien, as though covered by a diaphanous scrim. Nearby mud-hovels, back from the brink of the hill, stood sharply stereoscopic, in contrast to the mirage-like city. But there was ballast to this fantasy. Donovan pointed out an obsolete anti-aircraft battery, not a hundred yards behind us, manned only by a caretaker; and Polk pointed out that the caretaker's little boy was throwing stones at us. In addition to being hungry, we now felt unwanted, and returned to the jeep for the trip back.

Donovan's Descent, for that is what this mad journey must be called, was a test even for his jeep, a machine made to be hardy. So wildly did we bounce and jounce that the spare tire fell off, the loss being discovered by Bland, our tail gunner, only because he checked to see whether we had one, if, as seemed imminent, a tire should be punctured by one of the sharp rocks strewing out path. Donovan turned the jeep around in a slithering maneuver, climbed back for a mile, and found the spare just off the road.

Meanwhile, back at the flat, a group of Arabian singers had arrived to entertain Marcelle's guests. Three women and four children, wailing and cantillating, beating drums and gourds, filling the night with shrill songs. Under the light of kerosene and gasoline lamps, we ate the food of the realm, buffet style, and kept the wire recorder warm for the festivities below.

The celebration, when it came along, was anti-climactic, and ranked well beneath Donovan's Descent. The setting surpassed the play. The Citadel and the Mohammed Ali Mosque were flood-lit; a searchlight, the kind used during the war to spot aircraft, was trained on the flag. The evening was clear, and warm with the radiations from the African desert stretching away on all sides. A faint breeze came off the swollen Nile. When fun-loving Farouk rode up the Fortress Road in a brick-red Cadillac, concerted automobile horns made a moderate din. It was all colorful under the amber moon of Ramadan, and everyone was expectant, but the show was badly stage-managed. The king did not choose to appear at a window or on a platform where everybody could see him; there was no roll of drums or blare of trumpets; a public-address loudspeaker, droning at intervals, gave out uninspired comments in Arabic, to which nobody listened; the lowering of the British and raising of the Egyptian flag was cheered, but not with the spirit of 1776, and suddenly the show was over and the crowd melted away. The theme of the evening had been Egypt's long-sought independence from the British, but perhaps there were too many Achmeds and Mohammeds and hubba-hubba boys and blind beggars, so willed by Allah, in that crowd.

A few days later we were to have gone to Palestine, but on the eve of our scheduled flight, the King David Hotel in Jerusalem was bombed, and the borders of Palestine were closed to all traf-fic. Because we had a tight schedule of airplane reservations all the way along the balance of the route, we could not wait for the situation in Palestine to relax, and had to press on to India. But George Polk felt that before we left Egypt, we should see some-thing of the terrain, so he arranged for Colonel Sandy McNown, military attaché to the American Legation, to fly us in an Army C45 Beechcraft. Bland and Polk were in the party, of course; as well as Ruth Hubbell, a USIS [United States Information Service] worker who was beautiful enough to be in a Swedish movie. We took off from Payne Field, and, with numerous circlings around objects of particular interest, flew north and east to Port Said and south along the Suez Canal. The grayish Sinai desert was dotted with airfields, ammunition depots, garrisons, and general junk of the late war. Near Ismailiya we saw below us, towering columns of smoke and flashes of exploding ammunition. McNown explained that the British were destroying surplus war materiel, in the process of dismantling installations as per agreement with the Egyptian government.

The Suez slices cleanly through its isthmus, marking off Africa from Asia. Shipping in the canal was light, with tankers and warships in a one-way traffic pattern, and a few freighters anchored in Great Bitter Lake. The two Bitter Lakes, Great and Little, form a hiatus in the arid wastes, and are as surprising to come upon as the Salton Sea in Southern California. We crossed Little Bitter, and continued down the final stretch of canal to the Gulf of Suez, apex of the Red Sea.

The city of Suez and its Port Taufiq looked like nothing much from the air, but the blue of the sea was vivid in the relentless sun. Mountains flanking the sea were of a reddish-purplish cast that had nothing to do with twilight, for the sun was still high. Polk ventured the harmless misinformation that the Red Sea took its name from the color of these mountains, a suggestion unanimously rejected by the rest of us.

We banked to the west, and McNown pointed us across the Arabian Desert. Sensing I was an aviation buff, he allowed me to take over the controls. There was little hazard in this, since the sky was empty of other aircraft, the ship was easy to handle, and anybody not suffering from middle ear disorders can keep a small plane level in the air. Soon the Nile came up on the horizon, a silver ribbon unfurling the last of its 4,145 miles from the Victoria Nyanza to the Mediterranean. We joined the river just below Helwan, and McNown had me swing the ship north to follow the Nile back toward Cairo. We flew over the step pyramid at Saqqara, earliest of the pyramids, and had a good, close, low-flying look at its crumbling magnificence. The Colonel took over again as we neared Gizeh, and descended until we were flying below the peak of Cheops—a spectacular way to see it. Then down river to Cairo proper, flying low enough to get a good look at four-motored BOAC flying boats moored in the river alongside feluccas that had not changed lines in a thousand years.

That night Lee and I packed for an early takeoff to India next morning. Polk and chauffeur picked us up before dawn, while it was still dark, and we drove to the aerodrome and checked in for a 6 a.m. departure aboard a converted York transport. I said goodbye to George Polk with regret. He had been a princely companion—bright, with a wry sense of humor, adventuresome, resourceful, hospitable. He had been a flyer in the Marines; he told me he had come out of the Midwest with an isolationist's ignorance about the world, and no sense of history; in a short time he had become one of the ablest correspondents anywhere in the world. He had a zest for living, bottomless curiosity, eagerness to learn, and a compulsion to get at the truth of any situation. He waved goodbye as Bland and I climbed the stairs to the York bomber. That was the last I saw of him.

[In May 1948 George Polk was murdered while covering the Greek Civil War between the right-wing government and the communists for CBS Radio. Polk, who had been critical of both sides, as well as of American policy, was found in Salonika Bay shot once at point-blank range in the back of the head. His hands and feet had been bound. The George Polk Award for outstanding radio and television journalism was created by a group of prominent American journalists just months after his death. The George Polk Awards, still presented annually, carry the same prestige in broadcast journalism as the Pulitzer Prize does in print journalism. Polk's murder remains unsolved.]

8

Nehru and Others
India

We came in low, and could see fires burning at a distance.

We left Cairo for India at dawn on a converted York bomber. There was a fleecy, broken overcast for the first hour, but desert heat burned every drop of moisture out of the sky by the time we were over Palestine, and we got a clear look at the Dead Sea as we crossed it on a diagonal. It looked very dead indeed, deader than Death Valley, which works hard at giving itself a mean, hellish reputation.

But out in the Near East, Death Valley would be a pleasant glade, a sort of Thames valley. At least it seemed that way as we flew over baleful mountains that frowned on the Dead Sea, crossed heat-prostrated Transjordan, and entered the glaring Syrian Desert, as cruel a landscape as one hopes never to be forced down in. The desert went on for hours (the York's top speed was 295 mph); then we picked up ugly swamps, and, at last, south of Baghdad, the Euphrates. It was wide, coiled like a colicky snake, and had a scummy green-gray complexion in the sizzling heat. Was this— *this*—the awesome river that had watered civilizations older than the Pyramids, that had flowed past Ur and Nippur and the Sumerian city-states, and Babylon and Kish? The Garden had been somewhere around here, and here Eve had listened to a snake in the grass. The course of the river had changed many times since then, almost as often as the costumes of Eve, and now the Euphrates was flowing sluggishly toward its confluence with the Tigris at Al Qurna, and our plane was lowering over marshes for Basra.

There was no air conditioning on planes, but while aloft at Basra the flight was comfortable. On the ground at Basra, the ship started to fry, and when we left it to go to a passenger's lounge a hundred yards distant, the noonday sun smote us. "The heat of Arabia," wrote T. E. Lawrence, "came out like a drawn sword and struck us speechless." That sun of Iraq (it was noon of a mid-August day) struck not like a sword, but a drop forge. I have been in the heat of Death Valley, which is bone-dry and therefore tolerable providing you are not sunbathing or playing tennis in it; but the heat of the Persian Gulf had enough humidity in it to make it malevolent. I could not wait to take off again. Soon we were flying over the Gulf itself. Its waters were a pale blue in that oven. Our course moved us gradually closer to that coast of Iran. Again hundreds of miles of fierce eroded mountains. We bore due east and soon sliced the very tip of Trucial Oman, a spectacularly rugged peninsula situated on the hook of the Saudi Arabian land mass. A tumble of desperate peaks, canyons, cliffs, fjords, rases and djebels.

We now flew over the Gulf of Oman, which is part of the Arabian Sea, which is part of the Indian Ocean; then over monotonous mountain country along the coast of Baluchistan and, as night fell, we came down in Karachi. [At that time, Karachi was Indian; the following year it became the capital of West Pakistan.] The Indians, like the Egyptians, were heady with the elixir of independence, and this took the form of fussy entrance routines. The plane was sprayed with DDT before we were allowed to get off. Then a health officer took the pulse of each passenger. As I had only two hours' sleep the night before, and had been flying for 12 hours in a plane whose motors made a crushing din because it was not insulated against sound, I was pleased to have a pulse at all. Neither Bland nor I showed symptoms of yellow fever or bubonic plague, and accordingly were admitted to Karachi for a night's sleep below lazy ceiling fans in rooms of the Palace Hotel. I was awakened at 5 a.m. and, with a cheerful Bland, all-unwitting of the joys remaining to us in India, we drove to the airport, a wartime American base, for the last leg of the flight to New Delhi some 700 miles away. The York that had carried us from Cairo was waiting, and we climbed aboard. Everything was the same, including our seats, but there was a new R.A.F. crew. The pilot stood at the cockpit door and made a little speech to the passengers. "I'm not sure what the weather is like upstairs," he said in a Cockney accent, "but we'll go up and take a look." It was a peculiar weather forecast, informal as bare feet.

Upstairs there was a thin overcast blanketing Karachi. It disappeared over the desert to the east, but when we were about 40 minutes out of New Delhi we began to meet ominous clouds, and by the time we were ready to land, a monsoon was in full blow. From 1000 feet the landing field was still visible through the rain, and one could clearly make out the runways. As we approached, the landing gear, which was stored overhead, came grinding down past the window. We were about to touch down when suddenly the pilot gunned the engines and we zoomed up into the storm and circled away from the aerodrome. Back up too went the landing gear. For ten minutes we droned through thickening clouds, then the field came in view again, and we once more approached the runway.

When the ship was only inches from the ground, the pilot, just as before, opened his throttle wide and we roared up and away to repeat his wide wheeling through the now quite insane storm. Four more times the big wheels were lowered, four more times we approached, four more times we pulled up without touching the runway, four more times the naked landing gear was retracted, four more times we circled through the blackening skies. Nobody spoke a word. No explanation from the cockpit. I was sure that something bad gone wrong with the wheels, since they did not appear to turn freely in the process of being lowered and raised, as they had done in the previous landings and takeoffs at Basra and Karachi. The hazard landing with the frozen brakes on a storm-swept runway was obvious to each passenger, but nobody as much as opened his mouth to speak.

Bland slumped in his chair, thinking of his wife and year-old daughter, whom he would never see again; I began to feel regrets for all the things undone, and the people to whom I had been unkind; I wrote in my mind the Associated Press account of the crash; I began dismally to calculate the effect the news would have on my family and friends; and I drew a bleak, pea-sized comfort out of the thought that I had left an elaborate insurance policy to be sliced up in interesting ways. Then my thoughts turned to resentment of the pilot who had been so casual about the weather upstairs. At the moment the wheels came down for the seventh time, the larboard one right past my window, and we came in for another of what was now established as a Grand Guignol approach. This time we touched the ground, rolled smoothly down the runway and came to a stop. What made the seventh descent any different from the first six, I had not the faintest idea, and I was too grateful for being in one piece to press inquiries.

At the Viceregal Palace in New Delhi, I paid a visit to the viceroy, the man ruling India in behalf of the so-called caretaker government, British Field Marshal Sir Archibald Percival Wavell. The palace is a massive, copper-domed Gibraltar of red sandstone, surrounded by gardens like a green moat. "Six miles of corridors, twelve miles of marble balustrades," a taxi driver told me by way of briefing. "World's largest throne room." I did not get to see the throne room, but I did see a good deal of the opulent carpeting, rich décor, marble trimming and trappings of empire. A chaprassi dressed in red, with a dagger at his belt, led me to a babu, who led me to an officer in the Grenadier Guards, who led me to a warmly paneled oval room at the end of which sat His Excellency behind a long carved table that doubled as a desk. He rose from his chair, extended his hand and smiled wanly.

Wavell is the man who pushed Rommel from Egypt to Bengasi at one point in the war, before Rommel pushed the British right back again. The poor gentleman has only one eye and he seemed to be shy and self-conscious about it. He listened silently to me for about ten minutes, and then spoke long and freely when I pointed some direct questions at him. The viceroy told me of India's problems—food, religions, deep traditional animosities. He picked up the morning paper in which several full-page announcements called for "Direct Action" on the part of Moslems. "How can there be unity in India," he asked, "when riots are precipitated over such incidents as a Hindu procession playing music as it passes a mosque? You'd think the Hindus might learn that this always annoys the Moslems, and the Moslems might learn to be less annoyed."

Before my appointment to meet the viceroy, I passed the Oxford Bookstore in Connaught Circus, and saw displayed a copy of an anthology of poetry he [Wavell] had edited. Its title, *Other Men's Flowers*, came from a sentence of Montaigne: "I have gathered a posie of other men's flowers, and nothing but the thread that binds them is my own." I picked the book up and brought it along on my interview. I had been much taken by the notes Wavell wrote in the anthology. They bore the stamp of a discerning and gifted writer. His brief introduction to the collection was at once charming and astounding with reminiscences such as, "'Horatius' was the earliest poem I got by heart, as a small boy. Admiring aunts used to give me threepence for reciting it from beginning to end; a wiser uncle gave me a sixpence to do nothing of the kind."

Throughout his notes there was much warmth and empathy, for instance, "[Thomas Beddoes] committed suicide at an early age and went to woo his ghosts; I wonder if he found them. For the sake of this beautiful lyric I hope that his dreams were made true and that he had untroubled rest." Wavell's collection ran some 420 pages and consisted of thousands of lines of verse. "I cannot claim that I can still repeat by heart all the poems in this anthology," he wrote. "I can safely claim that I once could." I told Wavell that I had recently read something that hewed to the core of the universal dream of One World and I quoted it: "May the spirit of adventure and self-sacrifice stay with us after the war, when we undertake the greatest adventure laid on the human race—to refashion a shattered world." I figured that any man who could memorize thousands of lines of other people's verse could certainly remember one of his own, and he did.

For the next 20 minutes we discussed poetry. I asked the viceroy, "Have you ever called on a poet for help in issuing orders or writing a state document or making a speech?" "Why yes, I quoted Horace in the first speech I made after coming to this office," Wavell replied. "Do you recall what you quoted?" "Yes," he said, "Keep your head when in difficulties—and refrain from excessive rejoicing when things go well."

Our next stop was All India Radio for a 10-minute recorded talk. A most pleasant and intelligent Moslem named Ashan Hugue, the public relations officer for the national radio headquarters, received me. I also met Igbal Singh, a bespectacled Sikh program executive. The AIR building is the finest I've seen since Norway and Denmark. Hugue and Singh were visibly pleased when I told them so.

That evening Lee and I were dinner guests of the U.S. Commissioner George Merrill, a State Department careerist who previously served in China and other eastern posts. He lived in the fabled splendor of the east, which has been somewhat well advertised by film and story. There were fine paintings and Oriental bric-a-brac. Not since I had dinner at Samuel Goldwyn's, the Viceroy of Beverly Hills, have I seen such fixings. (It's always comforting to know that our representatives in small countries like India are living so close to the people, and that they have a mere fifteen servants—which takes up the slack in unemployment, doesn't it?) Some of the rooms were air-conditioned and others were not. Too big. The meal was elaborate and beautifully served. It was Lee's birthday and we all drank a toast to him, each of us holding a small birthday cake as we did so.

On the day we were to take our wire recorder on the street to collect the voices of Indians, religious rioting broke out between Hindus and Moslems and our movements were blocked. In New Delhi we were restrained from entering the Old City. We were able, though, to interview Pandit Jawaharlal Nehru, India's Minister of

External Affairs and Commonwealth Relations, at the home of his nephew. Nehru was wearing the round white cap of the Indian National Congress Party. His sensitive face was drawn and sober. Nehru paler, grayer than I expected had just returned from Bombay and looked pretty tired. But he spoke quietly, eloquently, with a sure grasp of language and a smooth flow of ideas.

For almost an hour we talked on variety of subjects; first about Wendell Willkie, whose book *One World* he said he had read in prison, while under detention by the British for political reasons in 1942. We then discussed the international situation. I asked what he considered the greatest threat to peace:

> Well, I should say the greatest single threat at the present moment is the growing conflict between America and England on the one side—if you like to put them together—and the Soviet Union on the other . . . I believe that both parties are to blame for it, that they have done things that were wrong, and they have blamed the other party for doing the same thing, more or less.

Mr. Nehru spoke at length of India's problems, which he said were not formed suddenly, but were the accumulation of more than a hundred years. He had bitter words for the treatment of Indians in the Union of South Africa, whose racial policy he called "exactly on par with the Nazi doctrine." I asked him whether there was goodwill in India for the United States, and he replied:

> America is a country that attracts for many reasons. At any rate, it has attracted me, although I've never succeeded in reaching there yet. It is a vital country, a frank country, and it hasn't got all the legacies of past ages that drag other countries down and create complexes. On the other hand, one has a certain sense— at any rate, I have—of a certain roughness and toughness, a strange mixture of democracy and the highest pretensions of freedom—and the denial of that freedom, say to the Negroes, in America.
>
> That question often troubles us, because while we, ourselves, in this country have been guilty in the past, in the past ages, of

denying freedom to large numbers of our own people, and we are suffering for that. I think one of the causes for our downfall in India has been that we tried to suppress large numbers of our own people in the past. We want to get rid of that completely. And when we see that happening elsewhere, especially in a very advanced country like America, which attracts us so much, it is a painful thought, and it colors our opinions about these American declarations of freedom. Apparently freedom is meant for particular groups, not for all. But if you think of freedom for one world, then all this racialism or one race or one nation or one country being fundamentally superior to another, that has to be given up.

From the vantage point of this pleasant home in New Delhi, a city whose appearance suggests an American university campus more than an Asiatic government center, it was hard for me to imagine the vast Indian sub-continent of 700,000 villages, stretching away to all compass points, the stupendous poverty and struggle of its nearly 400 million people. These masses, like the relatively small population of Egypt, come within the bleak area of humanity that we call backward—backward because of no inherent lacks, but because of economic stagnation and total absence of opportunity.

I asked Pandit Nehru what recommendations he would make toward achieving the cooperative and united world of which Wendell Willkie spoke:

> Those countries that have power and influence in the world today should themselves give the lead in this matter and work out as rapidly as possible the idea of—call it the Four Freedoms, or what you like—that no nation, no people, should be subjected to another. No race should be considered an inferior race; and that the only way really for even the most advanced nations to carry on in the future is for backward nations to come up; to remove poverty, and to cooperate in the task of raising humanity as a whole.

Throughout our recording in a small reading room, Nehru's cousin and his cousin's young son listened attentively. Following the session, I had some fun recording the child and playing it back to him. Nehru saw us off, standing on the porch while we loaded equipment in the car.

That evening we went to a reception for a newly married couple that was taking place at the Imperial. There we met Andy Foreman, a *New York Post* correspondent. We were up until past midnight, sweating out the chore of packing. Up at 4:00 a.m. for a 6:00 a.m. departure. The drive to the airport was in an open-ended truck and it was very pleasant. Dawn was breaking as we pulled in, and a handsome spectacle it was.

We took off promptly and flew over rain-soaked, waterlogged fields. We came down at Cawnpore on the Ganges, which, like Allahabad, our next stop, is big enough to figure in a large scale world map. Took off again after a 10-minute stop and followed the heavily-flooded Ganges to Allahabad. There we had a good breakfast in a comfortable restaurant, and, no sooner had we finished our coffee, we were off again for Calcutta.

I napped for about an hour, off and on, something I have apparently learned to do on this junket. It turned out later that I would need it. Though the weather had been decent most of the way, we got caught in the typical monsoonery as we approached Calcutta. We came in low and could see fires burning at a distance. On landing at the military airbase and Dum Dum, we learned that it was impossible to establish even telephone contact with Calcutta because the riots that had started the previous Friday were continuing full force.

We were advised to remain at the airbase and told that the situation had gravely deteriorated. For six hours or so, dog-tired, we remained at Dum Dum. There, learning that a military convoy was going into the city soon, we threw our luggage and our fortunes on a big bus and ventured the trip. Six vehicles made up the complement—two buses, a jeep, and three armored cars—all manned by Tommies with Tommy guns.

The convoy got rolling at about 7 p.m., the light being very low by now. For miles we passed through streets of the worst squalor I have ever seen, and then—worse than squalor—bodies strewn over the roads, lying haphazardly and grotesquely, some of them already picked at by vultures, others bloated and stinking. Piles of rubbish from the fighting were strewn about, and now and then we passed an overturned, burned out vehicle. As we approached the center of the city we saw burning houses—some with flames still bright.

Our convoy landed us in due time at the Grand Hotel, whose narrow corridor-like lobby was jam-packed with military and civilian travelers, including some Dutch who had come in on a big KLM Skymaster while we were at Dum Dum. Tired and dripping, we got separate rooms and took baths, which left us just as hot and sticky as before.

Never have I seen a hotel as filthy as the Grand—dirt in the corners on the floor, cockroaches 2-inches long, no hot water, a foul tub, poorly lit, noisy, and altogether completely depressing. We had dinner in the unreal atmosphere of the Grand's dining room and hit the sack at 11:00.

The next day, Calcutta was still under martial law. We could get no transportation to carry our recording equipment. We had to watch our steps to avoid treading lightly on the corpses of slain rioters. A few feet from the hotel we saw further evidence of violence-smashed and looted stores, dead dogs in the gutter, and vultures over the refuse piles. With the help of the American Consulate, we went about the arduous business of getting transportation out of this tragic city.

We got to the Calcutta offices of China National Airlines right after dinner, although our flight, bound for Burma and China, was not scheduled to leave from Dum Dum, 15 miles away, until 4 the next morning. The curfew was on after dark, and the only vehicles about were British tanks and armored cars. The tally of the dead in the rioting had passed 3,000.

At 1 a.m. our convoy left for the aerodrome. We rode slowly through deserted streets, passing an occasional burned out house, its embers still glowing. Our headlights picked up corpses that had been lying on the highway for days, decomposing under the hot sun and steaming rains.

At Dum Dum, the passengers (Chinese, British, French, and ourselves—the only Americans) sat around in the open drinking a warm chemical solution named lemon pop. There were no stars, no moon, no breeze, no traffic, no conversation. Far off on the horizon was a red glow from freshly fired houses. A dog barked in the distance. I thought about the dead lying on the road. Whatever it was they wanted to prove, it was still unproven.

India was asleep. Four hundred million Indians, in their poverty and misery, were sleeping another night through. Eastward, beyond the Bay of Bengal and the mountains and jungles of Burma, 400 million Chinese were under the same blanket of darkness and privation. With the coming of the new day they would resume their huge struggle for existence. They too were fighting and killing each other. The civil war between the Communists and Nationalists was dragging on.

9

Under Heaven, Broken Family
China

Fifteen minutes Rest, + we were off to
See the Forbidden City.

The fare we paid to fly a dilapidated Curtis C46 cargo plane that
was never intended to haul passengers was our first experience
with the economy of China. It was three times steeper than the
tariff for first-class flying accommodations anywhere else in the
world. The distance between Calcutta and Shanghai was roughly
the same as between Los Angeles and New York, yet the cost of
excess luggage on this flight was $6.16 per pound, compared to 59
cents in the States. For deluxe rates we got a tramp of an aircraft:
canvas bucket seats arranged along the length of the cabin like
the seating plan of an old subway train; a total of eight windows
(three with holes in them); no drinking water; no toilet facilities;
no insulation; and no heating system. Even if the windows had
been sealed, there would have been no pressurization.

We took off an hour late, at 5 a.m.; and 20 minutes after leaving hot, sweaty Dum Dum, we were shivering. I was able to get
at sundries to keep me warm: on went an extra shirt; then, as it
got progressively colder, a jacket; a topcoat; a scarf. And I was still
cold. The same with Bland and the other passengers. We sat mute
and muffled, like refugees from Siberia. In this state we were not

in the mood to appreciate the rugged beauty of Burma's Arakan Mountains, nor the road to Mandalay that coiled to the south, nor the Irrawaddy River that glittered like a sword in a deep valley of its own making.

As we came down for a landing at Bhamo, only a few miles from the Chinese border and one of the checkpoints on the Burma Road, we peeled off clothing in reverse order. Though it was only 8:30 in the morning, the sun was already hot, and by the time we touched down, the cabin was an oven. The airport was as crude as our C46; it had been hacked out of a jungle not for frills or comforts, but for prosecution of a war. After breakfast, fuel, water and a shave, we were off again, and circled for 15 minutes above the airport, gaining altitude to clear a range to the east.

From Bhamo to Kunming we flew over wide and picturesque mountain terrain, forested slopes, red earth, coppery and silvery rock formations, uplands of crimson sandstone, and, at rare intervals, patches of terraced farmlands. As we descended for Kunming we flew over the northern extremity of a lake of spectacular beauty, the Kunyang Hai. There is a tingle in the sensation of seeing for the first time a landscape known to you only through paintings. I had always suspected no such country really existed—that it was idealized by Chinese and Japanese painters, stylized by the likes of Hiroshigo and Gyokudo and Hokusai because it was fun, good art, and a good living. But no, it was real; and there, slipping under the wings faster than I was willing, were scenes more delectable than the museum pieces.

The elevation on the ground at Kunming was over 6,000 feet, and the air was tonic. Gone the gnawing fatigue, gone the hangover of steaming and stinking Calcutta. It was spring on the high green plateau, not grueling summer, as everywhere else between Capricorn and Cancer. Stepping out of the plane was like setting foot on a planet whose atmosphere had been filtered, scented and mixed with a euphoric gas. I remember it as my Kunming Jag. It lasted through a hurried lunch of an amorphous but tasty stew at a lunch counter in the hangar, and then we were back as cargo again on a flying truck, and off for the thousand-mile stretch to

Hankow. Almost the entire route lay over desolate, tortured country, the widest east-west expanse of mountains I had ever seen. In the fading hours of the day we picked up the Yangtze as it wound around the feet of mountains and poured through the Yangtze Gorge, which we could see plainly from the modest altitude at which we were flying. Below the gorge, junks were sailing in a setting that again was right out of classical Chinese painting. Soon we reached the lake district, where a setting sun spilled rust in the waters of Tung Ting.

The airport at Hankow was big, bare and grassy, with nothing suggesting a city except a few spires barely visible on the horizon to the north. Once more it was hot and muggy. There was a refreshment stand on the edge of the runway, where Bland and I washed our faces in tea water, wolfed egg sandwiches, and got back on board for the last leg of this seemingly endless flight to Shanghai. There were two and a half hours of flying yet to go on this super-ventilated crate, and by now all the passengers were glassy-eyed with fatigue and punchy from the bone-rattling vibration of the motors.

We landed close to midnight in Shanghai, having lost three hours to Greenwich. Customs was the most disinterested yet—nobody asked to see our passports or baggage. The trip to town from the airport was on a bumpy open-backed bus whose driver stopped several times on the way to let people off and help them find the right address. He then chatted leisurely with bystanders. One passenger wandered off during such a stop, and the driver went down the street looking for him. After 36 sleepless hours, the last 18 in the air, with no idea of where of whether we might be put up in notoriously crowded Shanghai, Bland and I were hugely annoyed by the casual air of our driver, and conveyed this by signs and growls. But the Chinese passengers, every bit as tired as we, were uncomplaining. It was a detail, infinitesimally small and unimportant, of the quality of patience in people who for centuries have endured a great deal from those sitting in the driver's seats of China.

We landed at the Park Hotel, an UNRRA base, and made phone calls from there to Broadway Mansions, a tall apartment hotel with a highly unChinese name, where we got established in Room 1311. I tried vainly to get something to eat, then turned in deathly tired. We slept like waterlogged logs.

For a city to be noisier than Shanghai, it would have to be in a state of constant explosion. As we recorded on the Bund, the broad embankment along the Wangpoo River near Soocchow Road on a normal morning, the sound of busses, trucks, trams, ships, and hundreds of rickshaw boys was topped at one point by the striking of noon on the famous Customs House clock high above.

In the midst of this hubbub, Bill Costello, CBS Far Eastern correspondent, and I stood trying unsuccessfully to get shy Chinese people to speak. The inflation that in recent weeks had brought China to the verge of economic collapse was spiraling upward. A young boy, about 7, came up carrying tea in a copper kettle. He was selling it, per cup, at a gross round figure:

NC: What are you selling, son? What is it?

Boy: Tea.

NC: How much?

Boy: Hundred dollar.

NC: A hundred dollars?

Boy: Yuh.

Costello explained the devalued Chinese currency: "I once had a stack of Chinese paper money that measured about eight inches high—and it was worth only about 400 U.S. dollars . . . I'd say that a man could comfortably carry in his two hands about 1,000 U.S. dollars—which would be the equivalent of three and one-third million Chinese dollars." A movie ticket could be had for $1,500, a concert admission for $4,000, and a pair of American shoes for $50,000.

Shanghai's inflation was exceeded only by its congestion. To carry our equipment by jeep a distance of three short blocks in the center of the city took us an hour and ten minutes. We were on our way to see the mayor of Shanghai, K. C. Wu, to ask him about that very subject. We found him in his office in City Hall, a short, young, jovial, round-faced man with horn-rimmed glasses and an American education. He explained the acute housing shortage in the city: "Shanghai had a population of roughly three million and a half before the war. Now, although the census is not complete yet, I estimate the Shanghai population to be just a little bit below five million. And then, many houses [were] destroyed during the war. . . . Less houses, more population."

I asked Wu what he thought about the future of peace. His answer made no reference to the fighting between Guomintang and Communist armies a few hundred miles to the north. "Mutual distrust," he said, was the root of all evil. I asked what he thought the best remedy for this. His answer was general, and, in this respect, also typical of the statements of many leaders in China:

> I believe that everybody should show his cards on the table. Everybody should play fair. That's what I'm trying to do here in Shanghai. Shanghai is a sort of international city where you get all populations. But I think that as mayor of this city, we should lay our cards on the table. We try to give everybody—no matter what kind of nationality—the same kind of protection and the same kind of rights.

We left the mayor's office and headed back to Broadway Mansions. In a few short blocks there was a cross-section of the cosmopolitan character of the city: movie houses named Uptown, Rialto, and Paris; a Russian restaurant named Jeep; a sign in French; and music streaming out over a loudspeaker in a record shop boldly mixing Chinese and Brazilian motifs.

Shanghai most assuredly is not China any more than New York is America. But in some ways it is fairly representative. There were 46 newspapers in the city when we were there, but none had much of a circulation. The common man doesn't read because he can't read; and he can't read because there are no schools for him. In America we take for granted all kinds of things that are beyond the wildest imaginings of hundreds of millions in a country like China. In the United States a child is vaccinated for smallpox, diphtheria, and scarlet fever, and has a park to play in. None of that worth mentioning happens in China. In American cities we drink water from a tap. In Shanghai you'd no more think of doing that than you would think of swimming in typhoidal Soochow Creek. If a poor man in Shanghai is seized, let's say with appendicitis, he either gets over it or he dies. In these respects, Shanghai *is* China.

All of the attributes of medievalism—poverty, disease, ignorance, and squalor—are to be found side by side with wealth, education, art, and social refinement. This, at least, we observed in the three big cities we visited in Guomintang China as opposed to Communist China. There are two Chinas and we didn't get to see the second.

Unlike many of the Egyptians, the Chinese at least knew the big war was over. But they were too absorbed with day-to-day problems to worry about veto power, Greek elections, or trouble in Palestine. Not even at the cultural level of writers, artists, and actors was there much concern. In Nanking, Who Yi Kwan, of the Guomintang Central Cultural Commission, explained: "In these days, the life or the living conditions in China are so difficult that many cultural workers cannot think of anything else but their own problems. They have very little time to think of international things that are not very close to their own lives."

I found, as I went about meeting people in the cultural field, that I could get no more than general answers to specific questions. We visited a film studio and I talked for hours with actors and directors. Somehow, as though by gravitational force, the conversation kept returning to the movies. A very pretty actress, Miss Chang, spoke of her favorite Americans, "Humphrey Bogart, Charles Boyer, and Gary Cooper." Her director, Che Li Lo, did open up a bit, though. He told us the Chinese film industry was in a bad way. "Film production in China is difficult," he said, "because we don't have enough raw materials and equipment. And actors have to work at a salary set by the government."

Outspoken comment about the Guomintang government, either pro or con, was difficult to get. It was explained to me that liberals who were against both Communists and Guomintang, were having a hard time of it. The principal scandal during the time of our visit was the recent assassination of two leading liberal professors in Kunming. Both were graduates of American universities, non-Communists, and outspokenly critical of the regime of Chiang Kai-Shek, leader of the Guomintang Party. One of the eminent professors delivered a speech attacking certain policies of the Guomintang government and was shot in the street. The other scholar delivered a bitter oration at the funeral of his colleague and he too was shot—upon leaving the chapel. Liberals complained that they were caught in the middle; that without armies to back them up, as the Communists had, they were at the mercy of Guomintang extremists.

Strangely enough, within this turbulent situation, there was considerable homage on all sides to the ideal of One World, as set forth by Wendell Willkie. Scores of people with whom we talked had either met Willkie when he visited China in 1942 or had known about him. I was told a least 50 times by proud Chinese that the idea of One World had ancient beginnings on their soil, and the services of no less distinguished an exponent than Confucius.

A reception held at the International Club, hosted by the affable Minister of Information, Dr. Peng Pei, opened with this introduction: "Mr. Corwin, ladies and gentlemen, I'm very happy that you arrived at our Capital on the birthday of Confucius, who is the forerunner of the One World idea." And then Dr. H. H. Kung, himself a descendent of Confucius, explained that the Chinese equivalent of the phrase One World has been in circulation for centuries; that it was a popular motto to be found among the most honored inscriptions of public buildings. The title of Willkie's book *One World*, he said, "has been translated into Chinese as 'Chang Shai Ja," which literally means 'One Family Under Heaven.' "

The Chinese respect the motto "One Family Under Heaven." But unfortunately, China is itself by no means one family. Of the two Chinas, the bigger, representing roughly two-thirds of the country, is under the regime of Generalissimo Chiang-Kai-Shek, a regime that his enemies call a tyrannical dictatorship. The other third, centering in Shansi province, is in the hands of Chinese Communists, whose regime the Guomintang call equally bad names.

The two factions have been fighting for years, and until recently, the United States, through General Marshall, tried to mediate. That mission failed. Marshall placed the blame on both sides. Correspondents who had been in China for years could not agree on who was responsible. So, I certainly was in no position to make a decent estimate. I was not able to get to Communist-held territory, nor did I meet the Generalissimo himself.

I did, however, meet with the chief spokesman for the Communists in Nanking, General Chou-En Lie, a soldier and statesman famous in Chinese revolutionary history. We interviewed him at his small crowded house on the edge of Nanking. His personality was easily the most arresting of any person I'd met thus far in the city. He laughed frequently, flashing a great smile. He thought quickly and spoke well—if the translation by his interpreter was any indication.

He told us that the Chinese Communists had welcomed the coming of General Marshall to China as a mediator. He said that the early mediation was successful, but that Chiang-Kai Shek had violated agreements, and by doing so frustrated Marshall's work. He pinned the blame on Guomintang and was equally critical of American aid to Chiang-Kai Shek:

> I feel sure that the American people would never come to understand why, on the one hand, while the American government is mediating in the dispute, that on the other hand it is rendering all kinds of war supplies and materials to aid one of the two opposing parties that are fighting against each other. We are willing to cooperate with the American people, but we have to criticize the erroneous part of the American policy.

The following day our first appointment was with Dr. Wu Yu-Hsuen, president of National Central University. But when we arrived, about 25 minutes late, he had "gone." I was asked whether I'd like to see the dean instead, but I declined. We then went to see Dr. Chen Tien-Fang at the Central Institute of Political

Sciences, which is currently resuming operations in Nanking after a long absence due to Japs in Chung King. The school is enlarging and also changing its name to conform to the so-called cessation of one-partyism controlling public institutions. This, like so many other interviews here in China, was as dull as could be.

Later we went to the house of Ambassador Leighton Stuart. He was much older than I'd have expected and he showed the effects of his long internment by the Japs in Peiping—the story of which he told us with quiet and good-humored detail. He was surprisingly frank on the subject of his recent meetings with Chiang, saying that the Gimo had lately promised civil liberties "for all but the Communists"!

I was up before cockcrow for our 7 a.m. departure to Peiping [Beijing]. The flight was fast and pleasant and I used the time (3:30) to write letters. We were above the clouds most of the way and in a rainstorm. But the weather cleared about 100 miles south of Peiping and we had a good view of the Forbidden City as we flew in over the area.

We were met at the airport by a large delegation of Chinese, including the Minister of Information, newspaper and radio people, and our chief interpreter, Ming Tso. In two cars we drove into the city and registered at the Wagon Lits hotel—"the best suite in the best hotel," said Miss Tso. Fifteen minutes' rest and we were off to see the Forbidden City.

The grace and reasonableness of the plan of the city, the generous use of space, the good, clean use of tiles, the reds and golds and greens, gave me a lift. I could not help comparing it to the overbearing architectural colossi of Western culture—the palaces and cathedrals that weigh heavily on the eye and spirit. But also in my heart was mayhem for the principle of crushing aristocracy and exclusivity—the forbiddingness of the Forbidden City.

There was time enough after our tour to change for a cocktail party given in my honor by the Peiping Press Association at the Peking hotel. There were all manner of people in attendance. When it was all over, Lee and I repaired to the Wagon Lits for dinner.

The next morning Lee reported a sore throat. So I told him to quit work and go to the hotel and lie down. My first stop was for an abortive interview with General Li Tsung-Jen, director of the President's Field Headquarters in Peiping. It was abortive because the General's interpreter, a nearsighted colonel, was afraid of the written questions I'd submitted.

At noon I was tendered a luncheon by Mayor Hsung Pin at a beautiful palace named Ha Hua T'ing. Between appointments I visited a park called North Lake and climbed in the wicked heat to the top of a Buddhist shrine that overlooked most of the Forbidden City. For an hour I interviewed Dr. Hu Shih, former Ambassador to the United States and now president of the National University of Peking. At 5 p.m. I attended and addressed a tea given in my honor by the Sino-American Cultural Association.

When I got back to the hotel, I found that Lee had left his bed. So I went alone to dinner as the guest of General Cheng Kai-Ming, Commissioner of the Executive Headquarters. The meal, a simple thing of only 14 courses, was the most exquisite I have ever experienced. Lee was not back at the Wagon Lits when I returned, and for an hour I inspected and bargained with a Chinese merchant who was selling robes, and gowns, and jackets. Lee finally showed up trailing a lieutenant with whom he spent the evening. At 11:30—after I'd ordered him to bed!

The next day we visited the Temple of Heaven and the Summer Palace; the former I thought marvelous from the exterior and in its approaches. I was disappointed, though, at the cumbersomeness of its interior—especially the use of thick, heavy beams to break up the cylindrical effect of the dome. The Summer Palace, while brilliantly landscaped, I thought inferior to what I'd seen in the Forbidden City and the Temple of Heavens. I went on to a scheduled meeting of the Reporters Association of Peiping to give a short talk. I did, and it was not a very good one. Nevertheless, the meeting voted me an honorary membership in the Association.

It rained long and heavily; I went wearily back to the hotel, got into bed and snoozed for a bit. Then I dressed and went to dinner at the home of Walter Robertson, U.S. Commissioner at the American Embassy, a former bank president from Richmond, Virginia. Also present were two of his aides. The talk from Robertson took two courses—anti-Russian and anti-Yankees, circa the War Between the States. He still fought on, unwilling to accept Gettysburg as a setback for the Confederacy. At one point he took out of his wallet a clipping containing the quote from an early Lincoln speech on the Negro as inferior.

Ever since arriving in China we had heard a great deal about the so-called Executive Headquarters in Peiping. The ill-fated organization, set up by General Marshall, was a bold experiment in peacemaking and we went there to take a look—not knowing our visit would cause a minor incident.

The Executive Headquarters consisted of entire staffs in triplicate: Guomintang, Communist, and American personnel for each post, operating under three Commissioners. It served as a sort of fire brigade to put out smolderings wherever they occurred on the long incendiary front between Guomintang and Communist forces. Whenever trouble arose, one of 30 field teams was sent at once to the area and remained on the spot until the situation was cleared up.

Though the work of Headquarters was difficult, there was still hope for ultimate success at the time we were there. We recorded the three Commissioners: Walter Robertson for the United States, General Chang Kai-Ming for the Guomintang, and General Yeh Chien-Ying for the Communists. Robertson explained, "The United States members are participating as a third party in the role of mediator. It is being carried out by trial and error and is continuing through the sound judgment and willing cooperation of all participating members."

The recordings were made in Robertson's office and the opposing Guomintang and Communist commissioners chose not to be present while each other spoke. My questions, by prior agreement, were limited to the scope of positive accomplishments; principally whether the unity achieved at Headquarters could be broadened ultimately to the whole of China; whether from their experience as commissioners, they had any higher hope for the realization of One World; whether they had a message for Americans.

The Guomintang General, speaking through his own interpreter, said: "Each time a problem is resolved we establish added precedent, which will one day be the basis for the arbitration of disputes rather than resorting to armed conflict. I do not believe that Executive Headquarters has yet had the time to be accepted completely as a model because our principal problems have been primarily of a military nature. However, I state plainly and sincerely, that both our accomplishments and our mistakes will stand as a model in the world to come."

General Yeh, once chief of staff of the Chinese Red Army, began by saying that in the first months, Headquarters had been comparatively successful. "This," he said, "was mainly shown by the fact that civil war had ceased in a large part of China." But at this point the General departed from the agreed upon area of discussion. Yeh began a criticism of American policy: "The American government gave esteemed gifts to Guomintang of lend-lease and military supplies to enable Guomintang to wage a civil war, as well as using American Navy and Marines to support aggressing Guomintang troops. Such one-sided help cost the failure of General Marshall's mission. We hope that the American government will change its present double-edged policy."

Robertson shook his head in protest while Yeh was speaking, but made no comment until the General finished. Then, reddened and deeply agitated, he dressed Yeh down: "If you want to propagandize, you can issue that statement from Yenan. But it can't come from here. I for one am unwilling to sit here in Executive Headquarters and listen to an attack on my government in its role as mediator." While this was going on, his stooges had informed the Guomintang Commissioner and he rushed back and protested too. He demanded that the wire be left behind! Finally Lee got away with his wire on the false guarantee that we wouldn't use it.

In our brief stay in China, the distribution of our time was such that I talked with more officials and government leaders and less with common people than I had in other countries—although, of course, I saw the latter by the tens of thousands, which is easy to do in China, and took note of the conditions in which they lived. My own evidence is unimportant, but I think highly worthy of the record are a few excerpts of a letter I received from a friend of mine, Mrs. Mary Mumford, a woman of about 50 who was doing relief work in Henyang while we were in China. She wrote:

> No one who has not seen a famine can imagine the suffering and mass starvation. Hundreds of people wandering dazed and lost in the streets—many of them lying in the middle of the street dying of dysentery—many of them hobbling along with the most terrible leg ulcers covered with flies. The children were the most haunting—little animated skeletons looking old as the hills, the skin drawn back from teeth as if the mouth itself were going out before seeking food. The Chinese themselves seemed not to see them! I suppose they have grown accustomed to the sight of human suffering. The obstacles and frustrations of our work are unbelievable. . . . No supplies; then supplies and no trucks; then trucks and no gas; no communications; no water; no light—never any escape from the hideous tasks.

After the escape from Headquarters we drove to the airport—far from the city, near the Western Hills—for a 2 p.m. departure back to Shanghai. We had a good 25-cent lunch and then took off from a muddy field. The city was remarkable from the air, and with distance one could see the whole entity of Peiping within its walls—square—without much beyond. Flew over plains between high mountain systems and I was fascinated by the great numbers of villages scattered in every direction. After a short while, we flew over flooded areas of the Yellow River and then ran into overcast. When we outran it, we were over hilly, terraced country.

The plane droned on and approached the enormous mouths of the Yangtze, with its great islands of rich farm country. And as we lowered for a landing at Kiangwan, we flew over the confluence of the Yangtze and the Whangpoo, crowded with shipping. After the relative coolness of Peiping we roasted in the evening heat as we wangled transport into Shanghai and checked in at the Broadway Mansion.

After dinner I headed to station XMHA, a U.S. Army outfit broadcasting to the Shanghai area. I was to record an extemporaneous preface to a recording of *On a Note of Triumph*, which that station is planning to use on the final day of its existence, September 15, 1946. I was good, I thought.

I returned to Broadway Mansions to pack for a 5:30 a.m. rising—and damned if I didn't blow a fuse. This caused no end of confusion and delay before we could get an electrician to fix it. It was after 1 a.m. on this murderous, sweltering night that we finally turned in.

I was up, beaten and sore-eyed after less than three hours of sleep, and then back to the airport for the flight to Tokyo. We got to the field about 7:30 and were greeted by the news that we must have shots for "Jap B Encephalitis." We were briefed on Mae Wests [flotation vests] and were required to wear them on boarding the plane and for as high as 2,000 feet.

The plane, a 4-motored C54, was comfortable and not too crowded. I spent the first couple hours talking with an Army officer, a veterinary named Taplow, about health and politics in China. A fine fellow, but a tenor. In fact, he sang loudly while I was composing on the typewriter. "Not to show you I can sing," he explained. "I just have to." Taplow had recognized me from my pictures and confided that during the war he and his family used to worry lest I get drafted. He said he felt I was really needed by the country right where I was, in radio.

10

Big Archipelagos
Japan and The Philippines

Was Received by General MacArthur at his office in GHQ punctually at 12:30 pm.

As we flew over the southernmost Japanese islands, the skies cleared and we had a good view of the rugged mountain country of Shikoku and Honshu. We followed a straight beach for scores of miles, all the while sighting Fuji above clouds for as far as 115 miles. I went up to the cockpit to sight the old bird. The captain obligingly flew us right up to, over, and around Fuji—and it was one of the top thrills of all the flying I have ever done. The mountain's crater is tilted at a sharp angle, and so was the plane. The result was a fascinating geometrical-spatial-topographical orgy.

We continued over Yokohama and the Bay and across the heart of Tokyo, landing at Haneda Airport, a new base dredged out of the Bay. From Haneda we were driven by bus to the center of Tokyo and there were we picked up by Margaret Parton of the *New York Herald-Tribune* and transported by jeep to the Press Club, #1 Shimbua Alley.

Lee was quite ill by now and I was tired as hell. The next day Lee stayed in bed. The heat and humidity were fearful and I really couldn't do any work. I lay on my cot reading Waugh's *Black Mischief,* a novel he wrote in 1932, and not very good. In the evening I tagged along with CBS correspondent Bill Costello to Radio Tokyo for a 9 p.m. broadcast (8 a.m. in New York). But nobody showed up at KQW in San Francisco (5 a.m. there), so a technician in Tokyo recorded Bill's spot.

That night Bland was getting worse, complaining of a tight chest, and I was quite worried about him. In the morning the Army sent a doctor to see Lee at the Correspondents Club. While Lee rested in the afternoon, I went with Costello and Margaret Parton on a 2½ hour drive by sedan to the Fujiya Hotel, a splendid resort in the village of Miyanoshita, near the town of Odawara on Sagami Bay—the same bay where Halsey's fleet lay offshore for three days before entering Tokyo Bay. Margaret had dinner with us and then returned to Tokyo with the car while Bill and I stayed on.

I went to bed early, 10:30. It was cool enough for blankets and a busy brook, down from the mountains, gave a restful background to the night sounds.

The next day was a lazy one that included a session of teaching Costello the rudiments of chess. We had a Sukiyaki dinner amid political chatter and entertainment by Japanese performers. The following day too was low key. For the first time since Rome, I sunned myself, lying on a bench at the hotel's tennis court. The weather was perfect, the hills green, the water cold, the food good.

After lunch, Bill and I started walking and were offered a ride by a Marine driving a jeep. We accepted and went over a bumpy road to a high pass known to Americans as Longtail, but to the Japs as Nagao Pass. On the way, we passed through the drab little village of Sengaku and were afforded an excellent view of Lake Hakone. We drove through a tunnel and came out upon a prospect that included Fuji, some 20 or so miles away. Heavy clouds obscured the peak for most of the half hour we rested there, but every now and then we would get a good glimpse of her. What followed later were a whiskey-cola, a good dinner, some letter writing, a bit of reading into *Walden*, and an early bedtime—with the brook playing music to my weary ears and the night air making peace with my nostrils. We went back to Tokyo in the brilliant sunlit morning, reluctant to leave Fujiya.

I arranged to interview General Douglas MacArthur before we left Japan. He received Lee and me in his office in GHQ punctually at the appointed time of 12:30 p.m. MacArthur sat deep in his chair, his back to the light, in an attitude of complete relaxation. He smoked a pipe, and from time to time re-lit it as it went out. In a quiet voice he took off on what I had been advised beforehand would be his favorite subjects: the democratization of Japan and the menace of the Soviets. For 45 minutes the Supreme Commander ranged through these subjects and opinions:

- That Japan was "without problems."
- That democracy had taken firm root here; "Japan would vote to be a 49th state today."
- That Japs do not want regimentation.
- That the world is now divided on the vital and fateful issue of democracy vs. regimentation.
- That the Japs admire the U.S. for having beaten them; that they've had their fill of war; that the occupation is a tremendous success.
- That if the U.S. pulled out of Japan it would "create a vacuum" into which the Russians would quickly flow.
- That Stalin (pronounced Stay-lín) is a canny and clever old man; he is going to die (a safe enough guess) and that when he does, there will be nobody to hold the USSR together and its people will strike out for "freedom."
- That Stalin is not worried about China and Europe. He figures "communism is rolling in both places," but he has his eye on the Mediterranean because that's likely to be the area of most trouble.
- That Stalin is friendly to the Arabs, and that's the chief reason he's "backed out of Iran"—so as not to offend the Arabs, upon whom he is counting for the future.
- That the bureaucrats and part of the press at home don't understand the menace of Russia.

Right: George Polk (center) at dinner party in Cairo given by translator Marcelle Hitschmann (next to Polk).

Below: Pilot Col. Sandy McNown (L), Ruth Hubbell of USIS, Corwin, unidentified man, and Bland prepare for flight.

Above: Corwin takes control in mid-flight.

Left: Corwin with an Egyptian girl and toddler. The pyramids of Gizeh are in the background.

Corwin with Iqbal Singh (far right), program executive at All India Radio and two unidentified men.

Chinese shoemaker at work in the street.

Corwin interviews Manuel Roxas, President of the Philippines at the Malacanang Palace, between them is Julius Edelstein military attaché to the U.S. Ambassador.

Water rescue demonstration at Bondi Beach, Australia.

The

ABC

Weekly

NORMAN CORWIN'S
VISIT—PAGE 3

NEW WAR
BRIDES. SERIAL
FOR A.B.C.

JOURNAL OF THE AUSTRALIAN BROADCASTING COMMISSION
Registered in Australia for transmission by post as a newspaper.

Australian magazine cover

Corwin looks over Australian election returns.

Interviewing Australian dock workers

Corwin visits the Sydney Symphony

TELEPHONE: M 6991.
(10 LINES)

CABLE AND TELEGRAPHIC ADDRESS:
"ABCOM," SYDNEY.

AUSTRALIAN BROADCASTING COMMISSION.

264 PITT STREET.

REFERENCE_____

SYDNEY.

G.P.O. BOX 487 SYDNEY.

October 3, 1946

Dear Tommy:

This I write on the eve of my departure from Australia, headed
for New Zealand. This has been a particularly happy visit for me;
the reception in Australia was head and shoulders above that of any
other country along the route. The people are cordial, hospitable, and
most civilized, and the country is an exciting one to be in.

Tell your Dad that I got his letter addressed to Sydney, only
today, which is wonderfully lucky inasmuch as it would have missed
me had it arrived tomorrow.

You know, all the time I have been here, I didn't get to see a
kangaroo or a koala bear or the famous kookaburra bird. But I did
manage to take a 250-mile motor ride through the magnificent Blue
Mountains not far west of Sydney. These people spoke about wanting me
to come back here sometime, and I think I will....if ever I get the chance.

There is not time to tell you the many wonderful things I did and
saw here; that will wait till I get back. Maybe if you ask me, I will
be able to refresh your memory. One thing I'm especiallu interested in,
is whether you can recite by memocy the countries from which you've received
letters from me. In order, of course. Love to all,

Corwin's letter to nephew Tommy

Volcano Park, Hawaii

Greeting a young man in Fiji

Corwin arrives in California

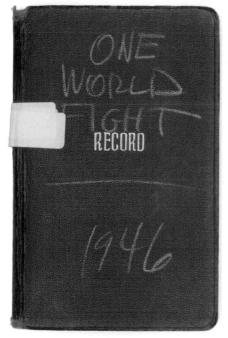

Above: Back in the States

Left: The One World Flight journal—hurriedly titled with misspelling—more than sixty years later

Pages of the journal

Close-up of journal

Corwin at work in his New York apartment.

Corwin directing in CBS studio

Corwin with Fiorello LaGuardia, the second recipient of the Wendell Willkie Award. LaGuardia did not live to take the trip.

One World Flight documentary series in production

With Carl Sandburg, circa 1950s

Norman Corwin in his nineties

- That the *Herald-Tribune*, which "used to be a good Republican paper," is now "solid pink" and it applauds everything the Soviets do and say; "its foreign editor, Joe Barnes, is an out-and-out Communist."
- That the *Chicago Sun* and *PM* are also Red papers.

I managed to intrude two or three questions at intervals when he was filling or lighting his pipe, but on one occasion he talked on, right through one of my questions. At length I suggested that we were taking up a good deal of his time and were probably colliding with his lunch period. MacArthur was silent, but his Public Information Officer, Brigadier General Frayne Baker, jumped in to say, "Not lunch, but an appointment with the Chief of Staff."

The next morning Lee and I took a jeep and set out to record what we could of a demonstration of 2,000 Japanese, mostly old folk, before the Soviet Embassy. The organization called itself "The Committee for the Acceleration of Repatriation of Japanese Prisoners of War." It was very quiet, in line with the recently expressed GHQ wishes on all such performances. Beyond a little shuffling of feet on the pavement, we got no useable sound out of it.

I had dinner that evening with Lee, Bill Costello, General Baker, Col. Larry Bunker, and a woman lawyer whose name escaped me. Among the evening's brightest gems was the intelligence that MacArthur was "more impressed" by his interview with me than anybody who'd ever seen him here in Tokyo. Baker also said that MacArthur was impressed by Lee's "attentiveness." Lee opened his mouth only to say "hello" and "goodbye." There was the usual anti-Russian talk too, of course. The next afternoon, Costello and I went to call on U.S. Ambassador George Acheson at his office. The man, an extraordinarily sour-looking but quite affable type, called MacArthur "a genius." Both Bill and I bore down on him quite a bit in our questions, but he answered without hesitation.

Costello took us over to the Diet Building, where we looked at the House of Peers and then crossed to the building of the Lower House to interview an English-speaking spokesman for the Communist Party. A soft-spoken bespectacled man whose training came the hard way—in Yenan. He told us of censorship recently exercised by the Japanese police and he said that the policy of the occupation had veered sharply to the right since May. We discussed a Communist Party newspaper that was on trial for publishing a cartoon caricaturing the Emperor.

After dinner we made a round of theatrical calls: to see an act of Gorki's *The Lower Depths* that was beautifully staged and acted at the Imperial Theater; a reel of a Japanese movie at Tokyo's biggest movie house; and a program of music and dancing by Okinawans—some of this we watched from backstage, where a young Okinawan generously stood *fanning* me.

The next day the friend of a friend from Seattle presented me with a Jap naval officer's sword—a handsome, heavy affair. Later we drove to the War Ministry to see a session of [Hideki] Tojo's trial, but the court had just adjourned (at 3 p.m. on Fridays) and we glimpsed only the blackened-out bus that was carrying the war criminals away. After a bite to eat, farewells, and a presentation of books to Costello and others, we were on our way to the Haneda airport by bus. The plane got away only 20 minutes late.

The pilot, one Richards, learned I was aboard and invited me to come up front. His father, it turns out, is chairman of the board of the DuMont television company. We chewed the fat at the navigator's station for a half hour before I went back to the cabin to enter my notes. Just as I felt tired enough to sleep, we started to come down for Okinawa. So, on went the Mae Wests and the safety belts. We made a bumpy landing and debarked at the Naba airport for 2½ hours.

To thousands of American boys this had been a last stop, but there was nothing around the airport now to indicate that a war had blown through here. It seemed, in the dead of the night, like any wayside fueling stop on a long flight; a shack or two, with a radio range, a small control tower, and nothing for the traveler to do but sit or stroll.

The moon was bright overhead, but off on the horizon, lightning jabbed the sky with silent flashings like the ghost of some bygone battle. I ambled around the field and found a ping-pong table on its last three legs that was long ago abandoned to the weather. I stretched out on it.

I wondered about dispatches that had been coming out of our next stop—reports of attacks by Philippine military police against a peasant movement in Central Luzon. When I left New York three months earlier, I was under the impression that Filipinos were rebuilding their country as fast as they could; that they were delighted with the independence granted to them by the United States; and were well started on their new nationhood. Whether or not this assumption was naïve or uninformed, I would soon find out because our C54 was all gassed up now and ready to take off for Manila, 900 miles away.

We landed at Nichols Field at 5:30 in the morning. The sun had barely edged over the horizon and it was already hot. There was no provision at the terminal to handle passengers or baggage, no transportation into the city. We hailed a truck, hopped on, and rode in. The ride was kidney crushing—at one point my coat, jacket, and binoculars fell right out. But finally we pulled into the Manila hotel.

I took an improvised shower with cold water in a common bathroom because our room wasn't ready. I awakened our much-heralded contact here. He was fairly fuzzy about the whole deal—didn't know my first name or how to spell my last—but he did manage to get us over to the Army & Navy Club for breakfast.

It was a ragged entrance that turned out to be fairly representative of the state of Manila, both on the surface and inwardly. For one thing, the city is, next to Warsaw among nation's capitals, in the worst shambles of the war. Its government buildings, once reminiscent of the solid, conservative and dignified architecture of Washington, D.C., are now heaps of rubble—gutted, twisted, sprawling. Bill Sanford of the State Department explained to us why the work of rehabilitation was going so slowly: "Beneath these ruins there are still many, many Japanese dead, which have been unable to be removed, simply because of this terrific destruction." We passed a number of shattered churches and I asked Frank Trinidad, a Filipino, whether any of the churches were left standing after the city was liberated. "Well, they're not churches anymore in the sense that you could hold Masses in them," he said. "All that are left are walls."

As we approached the Pasig River, which bisects Manila, traffic thickened by the yard. The American Army Forces of the Western Pacific (AFWESPAC) had released for sale thousands of jeeps, and these had been converted into vehicles called "jeepneys." They became the main transportation of the city and did the work of streetcars, busses, and taxis. But there were so many of them trying to cross the river, and so few bridges, that congestion was almost as bad as in Shanghai.

In two unfortunate aspects, Manila resembles Warsaw. First, the city is a total wreck; second, it is being rebuilt slowly and painfully—and by hand. We saw no modern construction equipment anywhere. Wherever you went, men were hammering, but I did not *once* see a riveting machine, a steam shovel, a bulldozer, or a tractor. As with Warsaw, the prospect of rebuilding Manila is one that must be thought of not in terms of a year or two, but of a generation.

One of the best descriptions of the conditions in the third month of the Philippine Republic came from its president, Manuel Roxas, "A large number of people are unemployed; homes, mills, shops, stores, and factories are in shambles. Our public buildings, as you can see by looking out this window, are in utter ruin."

Mr. Roxas met us at the Malacanan Palace, in an immense, wood-paneled, air-conditioned room. He wore a plain, undecorated khaki uniform. In the center of his desk, flanked by miniature flags of the United States and the Philippine Republic, was a statuette of Franklin D. Roosevelt.

He affected a knowledge of me and my work and was altogether modest and obliging. He sent for drinks and we sat around gabbing for well over an hour—about American politics, the outlook for 1948, his experiences with the Japs, and Tom Dewey.

It was cool and comfortable in the president's office, but outside it was hot and humid; thunderheads were piling up east of the city. Also piling up inside and outside of the country was public opinion—opinion pro and con about the man who sat across the desk from me. To his enemies he was a collaborator with the Japanese; a dictator who was using fascist tactics against his own people; to his admirers, he was a democratic, patriotic, heroic and wise leader.

One of Roxas's outspoken supporters is Paul V. McNutt, the last governor of the Philippines as a territory of the United States and, after its independence, our first ambassador to the Philippine Islands. I met him at the Embassy. He was a big, handsome, prematurely white-haired man who freely fell in with the idea of informality. McNutt's right arm was in a sling—bursitis. Of all the public figures we'd interviewed, he had the best voice and registered most clearly on our recorder. "I've dealt with many public officials in my life," McNutt said. "I've never dealt with anyone on a more satisfactory basis than President Roxas. He is a dynamic and wise leader. His people are accustomed to following leadership. They will do well to follow his."

But not long before our visit, former Secretary of the Interior Harold Ickes had publicly attacked the Roxas government as "a fascist dictatorship under which a newly liberated people is being shackled." He charged that the Roxas administration, in refusing to seat eight opposition congressmen who had been elected in Central Luzon, had given what he called "proof of its anti-democratic character," and he went on to charge that the undemocratic aims and program of Roxas had the sympathetic support of American army and government representatives.

Whether or not this was true, there was no question about the shooting in Central Luzon. An organization of peasants named the Hukbalahaps, who had fought as guerillas against the Japanese, had made demands for land reform and expressed generally sharp opposition to Roxas. They were in possession of small arms, which they had kept after the anti-Japanese fighting, and Roxas demanded that these be surrendered. There had been some nasty fighting north of Manila between government MP's and the Hukbalahaps, and it was still going on.

The republic was an infant, the youngest in the world, and its problems were many and sore. Apart from the civil war in

Central Luzon, the unemployment of which the president had spoken was clearly apparent on the streets of Manila and in the depressed condition of its people. While we were there, a crime wave was sweeping the city. That very morning Bill Sanford told us two jeeps belonging to the State Department had been stolen from a parking lot. Filipino veterans were charging that they'd been badly let down by Washington on the matter of veterans' rights.

The morale of American troops was also a subject of deep concern. Relations between them and the Filipinos having suffered to the extent that General MacArthur issued a statement pointing to what he called "the irresponsibility of a few American soldiers" and "the nationalistic feeling" of Filipinos. General Carlos Romulo, Philippine delegate to the United Nations, said publicly that he was "grieved to observe the extent to which Filipino-American relations have deteriorated."

As I went about querying people at random, I found that some Filipinos had misgivings about independence and blamed it for the growing unemployment. A college student explained, "Right after the independence, when America took away the sovereignty over the Islands, most of the people who were employed by the United States Army were thrown out of work."

I heard a radio from across the street. There were four radio stations in Manila and they followed the American pattern closely. Some of their daily programs were named "Early Bird," "Health Club," "Shopping Guide," "Philippine Homemakers' Club," "Swing Session," "True Confessions with Aunt Patricia," and "Bridge to Dreamland." I heard very little Spanish or Tagalog spoken, except on occasional news broadcasts. The cultural life of the city seemed to be pretty much confined to radio, press, and films, and in this respect was little different from that of any medium-sized American city. The same movies were playing, the newspapers used the American wire services, and the dance bands played the pop tunes current in New York.

There was, however, great individuality in the press. Some of the more colorful political criticism, for example, came from a columnist named Carlos Sison who was running a series of columns in *The Star Reporter* under the bold heading "People of the Philippines versus Manuel A. Roxas for the Crime of Treason." The columns consisted of an imaginary trial in which the president was submitted to cross-examination, with satirically self-incriminating answers. Ambassador McNutt was the Number Two target of the anti-Roxas factions and he was constantly figuring in political columns and editorials.

We took our microphone around the city to meet more of the people and ask them what they thought of the chance of peace. In most of the war-shattered cities we had visited, there was a great weariness with war and a powerful reaction against the suggestion of another one at any time. But here in this city that had been savagely attacked by a fascist power, and cruelly treated under Japanese occupation, I found stray Filipinos thirsting for another war—not against their old enemies, but against a former ally. A housewife and mother told us, "I am going to finish Russia right now."

NC: Are you afraid of the Russians?

Housewife: Ya, I am afraid of the Russians.

NC: Why?

Housewife: It is a big nation to be afraid of. Russia has an atomic bomb right now.

NC: How do you know?

Housewife: It is in the newspaper.

NC: What newspaper?

Housewife: Every newspaper.

NC: I haven't seen it in any newspaper.

Housewife: Every newspaper says that Russia has discovered the secret of the atomic bomb.

There were several views along that order, based on that level of information. One of the more moderate responses was from a young clerk who thought perhaps there might be another war. He added, though, "Once you can forestall a war, there is a probability that it will be forestalled forever."

As in other countries, we were at no time attempting a poll of opinion, but from those we did interview in Manila, I gathered that they were vaguely afraid of communism growing up inside their country; they seemed evenly divided in their sympathies for the Hukbalahaps; they professed to be largely pro-American, but not that largely pro-Roxas. There were deviations from this, of course, such as the estimate of conditions in the Philippines made by Mrs. Benedict Orel, wife of an American businessman:

> I think that for the first time I've seen what imperialism means and what fascism means as far as disturbing the day-to-day living of the people. We in the United States have it very easy. When we attend a meeting at night, we don't attend it with a pistol to protect ourselves, we don't have to be chaperoned; the girls aren't afraid to return home on the streets. But here it's different. When you leave your home, you don't know if you're returning to your home.

We also spoke with Dr. Vicente Lava, a prominent scientist with a doctorate from Columbia University, who was deeply disturbed by the state of the Philippines and the world. I interviewed him at his home in the countryside:

> All I know is that certain things are done in the Philippines along fascist or semi-fascist lines. Lack of civil rights, people cannot meet, people are driven away from their homes, people are tortured, and they're imprisoned without warrants of arrest, many of them killed. . . . There is no way out for people except to fight and defend themselves.

On the subject of peace and war, Dr. Lava said that he had prophesied the last war, even to the point of its being started in the Pacific by the Japanese, but he did not believe there would be a third world war. I asked whether he thought it possible that we might achieve the One World of Wendell Willkie's ideal within four or five generations.

"Four or five generations would mean around about 120 to 150 years, eh? I think we can have it."

One bright afternoon we set out for Corregidor, the tadpole-shaped island of terrible memory guarding the mouth of Manila Bay. We boarded an Army watercraft by the plain-Jane designation of QB-12, powered by two Packard motors. After an hour and a half of sailing under cloud formations that wreathed the hills of Cavite and Bataan, we pulled in at the North Dock of Corregidor, and transferred to a jeep for a tour of the island.

Here, mute, scarred and rusting, were the batteries that had so tenaciously defended the island, their concrete emplacements chipped, cracked, gouged. Here was Malinta Tunnel, dusty, dank, overrun by big shiny cockroaches. Here the arterial tunnels, the laterals, which had served as hospital and mess; the MacArthur tunnel; the accommodation at the open end of the main tunnel where an ailing President Quezon was lodged for easier breathing.

Nothing I had seen on this trip, save the ruins of the Warsaw Ghetto, moved me so much as Corregidor. I realized then, as so many times before, how terrible is the gap between the reality of an event and the concept of it in the imagination. Twelve thousand civilian and military personnel had been packed into this dungeon-like tunnel; 1,500 of them were hospitalized in a wing that was just as filled with dust and smoke, just as jarred and shaken, thumped and pounded by the endless bombardment, as the rest of Malinta.

Up from the tunnel, we climbed to the Old Spanish lighthouse, which is like a grace note on the rugged head of the tadpole. Inside were tiles dated 1836, unshaken by the shelling. From the tip of the lighthouse one could see Bataan, and doughty Fort Drum, shaped like a battleship. Its impenetrable turreted guns had kept up a steady harassment of Japanese positions on Bataan even when it was plastered by more than 1,000 direct hits daily. Isolated, cornered, a sitting target, it was never silenced throughout the long, harrowing siege; its guns kept firing until five minutes before the surrender. Old Drum was the essence of defiance.

Sharp in the strong light as we looked over the Bay, was Caballo Island in South Channel. In the waters between Corregidor and Caballo, one day after the Japanese had encircled Manila, 16,000,000 silver pesos were loaded on a barge and dumped to forestall enemy capture. Divers reclaimed them after the war. What could not be reclaimed were the dead of Corregidor. They rested in a sad and simple burying ground, Americans and Filipinos alike. Beyond the graves, the jungle had begun to cover the scars and reweave the matting for the battered earth. To the east, storm clouds were gathering—yellowish, with a red cast on low-hanging clouds, although the sun was still hours from setting. It was a brooding and ominous sky.

I wished that I had the blood of a poet of old, the kind who could take a scrap of paper from his pocket and write a commemorative ode on the spot. Instead, I picked up a few cartridges and shells and bits of rusting shrapnel lying on the ground at my feet and returned with the others to the QB-12. The storm passed in a mutter of thunder and distant veils of rain. A fugitive breeze parleyed briefly and was gone.

On our return Lee took off for the routine of checking our luggage for the flight to Australia. He encountered an almost vicious insolence on the part of an ATC [Air Traffic Control] sergeant named Eckstein—a brush that was to have repercussions not many hours later. I held a press conference for a handful of people at USIS [United States Information Service], and then we drove directly to Ambassador McNutt's house for dinner. The chatter was enjoyable, largely because it was non-political. There were movies—16 mm—after coffee and we stayed for a few reels. Then I finished packing and hit the sack.

We were up at 1:30 a.m. and off to Nichols Field by 1:55. And then began what was by far the most unpleasant experience of this whole trip. The ATC personnel had apparently been tipped off by Eckstein to give us the works. They charged we had not shown up on time and removed us from the manifest. I had sharp and heated words with a tedious snot named Corporal Jennings, an unidentified sergeant, and a Captain Keebler, pilot of the ship. I phoned and awakened Col. Hurd, trying to enlist his aid and the plane's departure was delayed by 45 minutes while the issue was wrangled.

The crux of the matter, at length, was that though they had removed us from the ship, they refused to remove our baggage. Luckily for us, our driver Bernardo loyally remained at the field, otherwise we'd have no transportation back. I slept only an hour—and that with the help of a pill—and was up and about with determination and indignation. We told our story to Bill Sanford and we drafted a "dispatch" bearing McNutt's name, protesting the indignity.

The next morning we worked on alternate air reservations out of Manila. After lunch at the Army & Navy Club we learned that the ATC wanted to know if we would "care to be added to the manifest" of a flight going to Australia at 6:00 the following morning. I enjoyed a good dinner with Sanford and Lee at a restaurant named The New Europe. In the short space of 36 hours we found ourselves able to laugh uproariously at certain aspects of the Nichols Field incident, which somehow attests to the resiliency of humor in the average man.

We took off at 6 a.m. on seats that had been "reserved" for us. The flight was pleasant, not too crowded with only about 20 passengers. We flew over two or three of the Philippine Islands, then out across the Zulu Sea, and on down by the Celebes. I at last tackled a piece I promised to do for Freedom House, and got started on it north of the equator; but will be finishing it well south of the same, as the lawyers say.

Somewhere over the Haymaker group, we flew over a volcano, but the first really formidable hunk of island whose identity I was able to get from the navigator, was Obi Major—green, mountainous, rugged. I identified the little island of Gomoemoe just south of it on our course. Then I tired of the sport and lay me down on the floor near the door. I tried to sleep, but succeeded only in resting my eyes. At about 5:30 p.m., I picked up Melville Island off the northwestern coast of Australia. Flat, green, dense. And an Aussie aboard tells me it abounds with brown alligators—or was it brown sharks?

Reverse Spring
Australia

The cool atmosphere after the sticky tropics gave me a lightness of heart

We landed at the much-damaged port of Darwin at dusk. There was a calmness about the evening that was restful after the hours of grinding in the air. We clambered aboard a long truck that resembled a flattop in its deck acreage and sat in camp chairs for the ride to town. The stars were out by now, and the sky seemed soft and brilliant. Our flight from the Philippine Islands to Australia took us from the first day of autumn to the second day of spring. It was a routine run, a pushover, taking only a day and a night to reverse seasons.

After a good dinner of steak and eggs at a Darwin restaurant, we got back on the strange truck and returned to the airfield for the flight to Brisbane. I found a place to stretch out and went to sleep.

I arose to find the cabin flooded with the red light of dawn. My outlook on life was not as rosy as my outlook on Australia, for I was dirty, bearded, and drunk with the roar of motors. The approach to Brisbane was magnificent, and we landed at a typical roomy airport. Representatives of the Ministry of Internal Affairs, the U.S. Consulate, and the Australian Broadcasting Commission met Lee and me. We were taken to the Lennon Hotel for breakfast and then a 4-hour sleep. I was up in mid-afternoon to do a 10-minute interview over the national radio network. Then, at dusk, back to the airport for the flight to Sydney. The lights of Newcastle were bright as we flew just east of her, out over the ocean. And a half hour later Sydney came into view— sparkling with blue and golden lights. We stepped off the plane into a nippy breeze and were greeted by Col. Charles Moses, Beryl Ross, Margaret McCallum of the Australian Broadcasting Commission, and several newspapermen. I gave a short interview and then we piled into a car and drove to town.

Moses had booked us into the Australian Club, a wonderfully situated, but extremely old-fashioned red brick building. I was a little disappointed with the small, cold rooms without baths, but the trip's biggest collection of mail was waiting for me here, which I read into the morning. When I went down to breakfast I learned that both morning newspapers carried photos of our arrival the night before on their front pages. Then I took a walk in the spacious and beautiful Palace Gardens, and along a splendid waterfront called Farm Cove. It was a crisp, sunny spring morning, and I found I was in love with Australia.

Sydney is a city to lift the heart: it has a deep serpentine harbor, or a series of them, with coves, creeks, bays, ferries, and a big steel-arch bridge, which made me think of Hell's Gate in New York. The city reminded me mostly of San Francisco, except that it's twice as big, its setting is less rugged and more complex, and it has more sunshine. The old parts of town have a European feeling, and some of the public buildings, especially Sydney University, could have been brought over from England. But its downtown area, the business district, has a modern and American look. There are wonderful parks and recreation grounds. And not far from the heart of the city are great sandy beaches and headlands of sandstone cliffs facing the sea.

That afternoon I held a press conference and was surprised by the big turnout of the local press. For an hour and a half they fired questions at me on a wide variety of subjects. Here I met

Sheila Sibley, a correspondent-columnist for the publication entitled *Woman*, who was highly attractive in a Jinx Falkenberg way. [Falkenberg was a popular pinup model, actress, and radio talk-show hostess in the WWII era.]

Australia's national election fell across our calendar, and the labor government was returned without any great contest. But we had the chance to witness the political system in action. We visited Election Headquarters for the ABC radio coverage and we also went to the main counting room at the Post Office Building. It all seemed very quiet and minor in comparison with American elections.

One feature of the Australian system that's worthy of note is compulsory voting. If a voter there does not exercise this prime function and duty of citizenship, he's fined. Moreover, the names of candidates on Australian ballots are printed without party designation or affiliation. It is assumed that the electors should be sufficiently acquainted with the names and qualifications of candidates by the time they reach the polls. The emphasis is removed from the party machine and instead placed on the individual.

They insist on keeping their election campaigns safe from knavery in the closing hour. No campaigning may be done on radio or elsewhere in the two days prior to elections. This, they say, is to prevent any unfair or illegal last-minute trick, to which the opposition might not have time to reply. On Election Day, early returns are never announced until after polls are closed, in order not to influence undecided voters.

Australia, I found, is a young country whose frontier days are not yet over. Her people have the toughness and vitality that go with youth; and although they're friendly and hospitable, they're also independent, outspoken, and proud. I had not been in Sydney more than a day when I ran into expression of this quality.

I stood with a microphone at the side of a cargo ship named *Corinda*. She was taking wool and rubber tires, but most of the work stopped when we showed up. One man, named Bob Robertson, introduced himself as the leading Bible lecturer of the domain. He said that what was needed in Australia and the world was practical Christianity, which he then went on to define.

Robertson: There is a difference between Christ's Christianity and the exploiters' Christianity, and that has to a great extent been one of the sources of the discontent that has prevailed among the peoples of the world.

NC: That is very clear to me. Tell me; are you one of the workers here?

Robertson: Yes, I'm a member of the aristocracy of the working class. That's the Waterside Workers Federation, and we're looked upon as the aristocracy because we give leads in matters of progress that affect the workers.

A tough little dockhand edged up to me and told me that as far as he was concerned, the Americans had it all over the British: "In the three years of their stay in Australia, I think Americans have done what England hasn't endeavored to do in 150 years."

Not far from this dock was the district familiar to so many American boys who were stationed in, or went through Sydney during the war—the district of Woolloomooloo, which I thought reminiscent of San Francisco's Embarcadero. The name Woolloomooloo was typical of the rolling and musical native names sprinkled throughout the Commonwealth—Katoomba, Wallangong, Marakooka, Murra Murra, Buckloo, Ergomango. The authors of these names, the native aborigines, were always present in language, but never in person; they were hundreds of miles away.

The stock of these workers on the waterfront, as most people in all civilized Australia, was white, and almost entirely British-descended. Yet I found some of them not as firmly attached to the British Commonwealth as I expected. One of these laborers startled me by saying: "Australia and America are two countries that in my opinion, and the opinion of a lot of people's here in Australia, should be united together as one great country." That remark was so unexpected that I passed the microphone around the group asking what status each man preferred—the tie with Britain, independence, or a federation with America. They answered in turn:

"America and Australia."

"Well, between America and Britain, I can't mention that because I'll get me head chopped off."

"Remain independent."

"Join with the United States."

"Me, I'd like to see England, America, and Australia all combined together."

Actually, the man who said he was afraid to choose for fear of getting his head chopped off was in the minority among the Australians we met. On every side of the political fence there was forthright speaking of the mind—a product of sharp political consciousness, something that is traditional in Australia. Almost everybody we met was ready to talk fluently about the world situation. For example, in Java there was fighting going on between the Dutch and the Indonesians. The waterside unions in Australia had come out in support of Indonesian independence and the longshoremen refused to load supplies for the Dutch. I asked one of the workmen to give me his thought on the situation, which he did with remarkable clarity:

> I believe the majority of the Australian people support the view taken by the unions that the Indonesians have complete right to their independence as declared in the Atlantic Charter. The Australian people, at the time of the charter, declared their adherence to it. And, having declared adherence to that principle, (we) obviously are in support of the Indonesians claim; and there has been no public clamor that the waterside workers or any other union should assist the Dutch.

This nation is no mere debating society, though, or just a country of talkers. Australia fought a tough war. Seven out of every ten men between the ages of 18 and 35 had served in the armed forces. The casualties among them were proportionately twice as high as our own. And the veterans who returned had definite ideas—ideas they expressed with impressive facility. Bland took the wire recorder to a busy street corner in Sydney one day and intercepted people at random. He found a good deal of anti-fascist and sometimes pro-Russian opinion. One Sergeant Wood of the Australian army, home on terminal leave after four years and considerable action in the service, said, "I think that it's quite possible that fascism will rear its head again, not perhaps in the same nations, but in some other country; very easily so in the South American republics; it could be China . . . I should suggest to the British and the Americans principally to attempt not to oppose Russia on everything that Russia suggests, and to try to cooperate to a greater extent than they do at the moment."

A tolerant attitude toward Russia, though, did not mean an acceptance of Communism in Australia, from all we gathered. The Communists held a few seats in provincial governments, but did poorly in the national elections. Again and again we heard pleas for cooperation with the Russians rather than antagonism, and unity instead of insularity.

Many Australians expressed the opinion that their country is a natural and logical haven for millions of Europeans uprooted and displaced by war; that such stock, being polyglot, and made (as the victims of fascism usually are) of the best and not the worst elements of society, would enrich their commonwealth, just as the influx of European immigrants in the latter part of the 19th century brought to America new strength.

Among the mostly well-spoken opinions of Australians I was shocked to find some anti-Semitism surface, including the question from a ratty little fascist who wanted to know if I was making the trip "to glorify the Jew." I asked him whether he felt Hitler's policy against the Jews was justifiable and his stammering answer revealed his prejudice: "Well, the . . . I think that . . . he had a lot . . . that he had an axe to grind. I think that Hitler had an axe to grind. That's my personal opinion. I personally don't like Jews."

One evening I was the guest of honor at a tremendous reception at the Australian Hotel hosted by the Australian Broadcasting Commission. I stood at the entrance of the room with the chairman of ABC and his wife and we greeted guests as they came in.

Boyer stood on a chair to introduce me, and for a few minutes I addressed the group, likewise standing on a chair. Afterward, I mingled with the guests, exchanging usual pleasantries. One man, however, engaged me in a brisk discourse as to what I had "meant" by my remarks. "Absolutely meaningless," said he. I gave back, which was not too difficult to do since the man was drunk. The following day, I was again a guest of honor, this time at the Journalists Club. There was a turnout of about 70 reporters; I spoke on the responsibility of the press. I made it off the record and took the glove off the fist. I spent the rest of the afternoon at Broadcast House—the ABC offices on Pill Street. In the evening, a group of us went to Prince's, a superior nightclub with a good orchestra.

At every turn, the miraculous setting of Sydney improves. I took a two-hour drive along the shore country north of Sydney and returned toward dusk, just in time to appear on a children's radio program called *The Argonauts Club.* I gave the kids ten minutes of the best ad lib of which I am capable. Later, I received a marvelous letter from Sheila Sibley telling me about a hospital in town I should visit. I phoned to thank her and invited her to dinner.

During our stay, the Bondi Surf Club had scheduled a special exhibition of rescue work, and although a sudden "southerly burster" turned into a hard gale, I kept the date against my better instincts. By the time we got to Bondi, a first-class beach not far from the center of the city, the wind was blowing at about 70 miles per hour. Nevertheless, the men, dressed only in bathing suits, went through the drill. They were purple with cold. The wind blew so hard that I could barely keep my coat from sailing off my back, still five men manned a lifeboat and went crashing through the breakers. Four others did a rescue act, and another squad rigged lines—all in highly military fashion. The poor "victim" then had to be resuscitated by artificial respiration, which meant lying down on the cold sand and being squeezed half to death every five seconds. A torrential rain came out of the black sky and ended the exhibition. As soon as I could get away I dashed back to the city to finish work on my Town Hall presentation for that evening.

The cold rainy night kept some people away, but there was still a turnout of nearly 1,000 people at Town Hall to hear my reflections on the One World trip. To my total surprise, I learned later, the ABC, instead of fading me off at the half-hour limit, cancelled the following show—by a music critic—and ran my show overtime. The next day, at noon, I addressed a large group of University students, speaking extemporaneously. From there, without stopping for lunch, I drove out to Cinesound and made a 3-minute newsreel spot. It was the first time I've ever been before a 35mm. camera and under lights.

John Douglas, an agricultural expert for the ABC, took us to a sheep station in Romobogoo, beyond Bathurst, on a warm morning, but as we climbed the slow grade of a plain that lies between the city and the Blue Mountains, it grew cooler, and by the time we crossed the Hawksbury River it was right nippy. We stopped for a beer at a snazzy-looking hotel from which one can look eastward over a vast expanse of lush farmland. Then we drove through the mountains, stopping three or four times to enjoy a particularly fine view.

The mountains of Australia are geologically very old, hence rounded and not terribly high. In this part of the country they never go beyond the timberline—and are less rugged than the Adirondacks. Certain aspects of the country made me think of Colorado, others of the reddish soil and the scrub pine of New Mexico; still others of New England. At Katoomba we got off the road to see the Three Sisters, a sheer rock formation two or three thousand feet high.

Through the sharp spring sun we drove on to Bathurst. After interviewing workers at small factory that had been recently converted from the manufacture of small arms to sportswear, we checked into a little hotel that was cold and dreary. I was up early the next morning, soggy and groggy. I had a provincial breakfast and then walked the main street. There was a pull of nostalgia that comes to me every time I see a small town like this—not nostalgia, but the reverse of it—taking me back to my late adolescence in Greenfield, Massachusetts, where there was a Civil War

Monument in the park and a Veteran's Monument in front of the public library. Here there was a monument to the town's dead of the Boer war with South Africa, unveiled by Lord Kitchener in January 1910—for the Empire.

After recording some interviews inside a canning factory, we drove 25 miles to a sheep station beyond Rockley and pulled up at the ranch house that was built by early Australian convict labor. There we met a formidable character named Terry—huge, Falstaffian, voluble, and hearty. We had a spot of Vat 69 and told our Vatican story in connection therewith and then sat down to a heroic lunch of chops fresh off an open wood fire and a milk bread baked in heaven.

Here there were only a few thousand sheep of the 105 million in Australia. It was shearing season and a group of migratory shearers were on the job. They were a strong lot of men, as they have to be for this backbreaking job; mainly a quiet reserved bunch, as compared to the dockside workers. There was among them none of the hurly-burly animation we heard at the sheep auction.

This part of the country, though only a few hours from Sydney by road, was called "Black Blocks," the equivalent to our "backwoods" country. It was an area where movies came but once a year—yet the world and its problems were well known to Romobogoo. The tidings of war and peace; the news of Potsdam; Hiroshima; Bikini; Fulton, Missouri—all had made their way through the Blue Mountains and over the gum trees.

An old sheepherder named Rufflie—a bronze, thin, and wiry man whose sheep dog put on a great exhibition of corralling for us—had a kind of rustic wit that made me think of Vermonters I have known. He said he thought it was a pity the atomic bomb was ever discovered. Bland asked, "Now that we have it, what do you recommend that we do about it?" "Only one thing to do—let everybody have it."

Far from considerations of atomic energy, hundreds of miles off the west and north of this gently hilly sheep land, scattered in small reservations on deserts and in bleak bush country, live the aboriginals. They were a fading race of primitive, nomadic people who numbered about 300,000 at the time of the first white settlements, and who today are little more than 50,000. These, the native Australians, have been left largely to themselves in the 150 years during which Australia was being developed. They were left to their own resources, customs, totems, myths, birth rate and death rate, left to helplessness and inarticulateness—voiceless except for their songs.

The people, in some places as close to modern thriving cities as New York is to Chicago, are nevertheless as remote to the average white Australian as Eskimos are to a Bostonian. They are dying off through no persecution—there was never any of the cruel massacres or exploitation that went along with settling so many other primitive countries; they were never taken in slavery or maltreated. But they never have been accepted either, or given any sustained concern or encouragement; they have only the crudest health and educational services and no political entity. It seemed almost as if Australia had not yet had the time or interest to think of ways of stopping the decline of a people headed toward extinction. This is all the more surprising in view of the fact that in most respects Australia is progressive, fiercely democratic, imbued with a sense of equality, and ambitious to achieve the highest standards of social life for its seven million white people.

I did observe, though, that Australia was beginning to discover its great cultural potential, and this included a growing interest in aboriginal art. A hopeful sign. An aboriginal painter named Albert Namatjira was gaining fame and international acclaim for his breathtaking landscapes; a source a genuine pride for the Aussies.

It was my good fortune to spend some time with another important Australian painter. The iconoclastic portraitist William Dobell often distorts the features of his subjects in a way meant to reveal psychological insights. Some traditional critics take offense at his style. As we shared supper at the Australian Hotel, it struck me that he is mild and soft-spoken, far more modest and agreeable than one would assume from the hard wit and brilliance—and now and then, cynicism—of his paintings.

Music is central to the cultural life of Australia. They have symphony orchestras in each of five state capitals. In Melbourne, not long ago, 105,000 people packed the botanical gardens to hear a concert; the Sydney Symphony recently engaged American Eugene Goossens as its first resident conductor. New writers and composers are encouraged. For example, a composer named John Antill wrote a suite based on aboriginal music, and when the work was engaged for performance by the London Philharmonic, the people of Sydney contributed to a subscription fund raised by a Sydney newspaper to send Antill to England to hear the premier of the work.

This was no mere highbrow movement to bring culture to the people; it went deep within the government. This was confirmed for me by J. B. McKell, Premier of New South Wales who was soon to be elevated to Governor General of the country. Mr. McKell was born a butcher's son and became an accomplished boxer as a young man. He still has some of the nervous mannerisms of the game, including a broad sniff and eye blinking. But, as we lunched, he spoke knowingly and enthusiastically about the cultural program of the government: "Well, now on the side of music, we only a little while ago made available an amount of 200,000 pounds for the purpose of establishing a state orchestra."

He spoke with pride of the care taken to accommodate sparsely populated areas with devices such as traveling schools, correspondence courses, lending libraries, even itinerant orchestras and paintings: "Our idea is not only to get our orchestras to our country homes, but also we desire to get our pictures— whatever pictures we have—to the country towns. You see, we have developed what we call 'traveling art exhibitions' and periodically we take a number of pictures from our National Art Gallery in Sydney to respective country towns."

The interview with McKell was the last of our Australian visit. Afterward, there was a luncheon in my honor tendered by the ABC. I thought it would consist of a half dozen commissioners, but there were about 30 guests, including Australia's Deputy Prime Minister Herbert Evatt [who was later elected President of the General Assembly of the United Nations] and McClure Smith, the editor of *The Herald* who had been controversial for criticizing Neville Chamberlain's policy of appeasement. There were a number of toasts and "supports" of toasts. Evatt, who was seated to my right, introduced me and I spoke briefly.

The next morning we went down to one of the most beautiful harbors in Sydney to board a flying boat to New Zealand, 1,000 miles away. A reporter from *The Sun* was there, and he interviewed me while the photographer snapped us in conversation took pictures of the boarding of the tender that took us to the ship, which was a converted Sunderland. It was a two-decker with the massiveness of a Fifth Avenue bus—except that it was more graceful, and of course, faster. We had a glorious take-off, flying directly over the bridge and out past Bondi Beach. The coast was clear and sharp in the bright sunlight and we could see the cliffs of the north shore up to the vicinity of Palm Beach.

In a few minutes we were out over the Tasman Sea, and cold settled in for the rest of the run. Flew mostly atop an immense overcast. We had two meals on board and they were both good. My great adventure was shaving in a frigid lavatory; where the water was only slightly above freezing—and then, between fitful napping, I studied a map in an attempt to whittle my ignorance on the subject of our next stop.

12

Project Antipodes
New Zealand

Lee + I were received by the entire Cabinet, Including Prime Minister Peter Fraser.

The rocky coast of New Zealand appeared through the window. We flew in over rich, green, hilly farmlands, and in minutes we were circling the city of Auckland. From the air we could take in the full magnificence of its setting on a narrow isthmus between two harbors. And our clipper, with barely a ruffle, set us down in the choppy green water across the harbor from a dead volcano known by the native Maori name of Rangitoto.

We were met at customs by three newspapermen, a photographer, and two men from New Zealand Radio—Noel Palmer, representing the non-commercial system, and John Griffiths of 1ZB, one of the commercial stations. For a half hour we sat in a limousine while I was interviewed, then we drove to the Central Hotel. Over dinner in a chilled dining room, Griffiths explained to me the complex New Zealand radio system, whereby the government owns the commercial stations and takes their kitty.

The next morning we set out by car for Rotoria, 150 miles south and east. The day was fair and the country sparkling—a cross between New Hampshire and Old England. We drove through

174

the prosperous town of Hamilton, crossing the Waitato River and driving on to Cambridge for lunch at the main hotel.

The springless car jounced on merrily to Rotoria, the immediate approach to which was alongside a great lake ringed by mountains. After checking in at the Grand Hotel, we drove immediately to the thermal area at Waikerarera and gaped in wonder at the geysers, boiling springs, and little hot fumaroles on the banks of a cold-water mountain stream. We were guided by a famous Maori, Rangi—who talked the ass off all of us. In the party was the Chief Ranger of the area, one Pickinson, an Empire type.

Between the geysers and dinner, we drove out to look at three crater lakes, close to each other but at different levels, and a grim dead volcano that in the 1880s had blown its head off and buried alive a little village a few miles away. After dinner, we went to the municipal auditorium to record part of a Maori concert, which luckily for us, happened to be the opener of a weekly series on Saturday nights. The smell of sulphur is strong in the town, especially when the wind blows off the geysers.

We drove over a 2,000-foot mountain the next day to visit a trout farm run by a private individual for the tourist trade. Then we headed north and I rode, sleepily, mostly through rain, to Auckland. There I immediately went to 1ZB and worked on a script of my evening broadcast.

At 9:30 p.m., a peak hour, over every station in the country, I broadcast for 35 minutes before a studio audience, using material from here and there, spliced together with some new stuff on New Zealand. I went back to the Central Hotel, where I shared a room with Lee, and packed for the Wellington trip tomorrow.

It took us an hour's slow bus ride to the airport. During the flight, clouds mainly obscured the ground, but we did get to see the snow-capped peaks lying north and east of Wellington. We landed at Paraparaumu, where we were met by a radioman, William Yates, and a garrulous but witty and pleasant old duffer named Owen Gillespie, who was attached to the Prime Minister's office. We got settled in the hotel, had lunch, and were off about our business.

The first stop was a veterans' rehabilitation center, where we inspected woodwork, jewelry, printing, carpentering, and other departments. Also saw some boys—amputees—who were getting fitted for artificial limbs. We then drove to a windy hilltop overlooking the richly endowed harbor of the city, and its rugged mountains all about. My beret again came in handy. The city I thought was one of the most attractive in the world, comparable to San Francisco in the extent of its waters, and the steepness of its streets.

Back at the hotel I had time for a 30-minute rest under a quilt before dinner. Then we went by car to Miramar to watch some documentary films at the national film studios. These I found nicely made, though slightly crude in some aspects, especially in the introduction of comic relief for perfectly straightforward material. After an hour or so of screening, I was invited to make a sound film for distribution three or more weeks hence. This, the second such film I've made (the first in Sydney) I found difficult.

Another place we visited in Wellington was an average public school named Rongotai, a Maori word meaning "sound of the sea." It was a secondary school for boys, in what was described to me as a "lower-middle-class" section of the city. Its pupils were remarkable—healthy, smart, and well informed. One of the boys we picked at random to interview was 14-year old Norman Major, who is as bright as a nova. We spoke as his schoolmates crowded around:

NC: What books have you been reading lately?

Major: Uh, *Bonin*—it's a novel on the expansion of Japan late in the last century.

NC: Do you go to the movies?

Major: Oh, very occasionally.

NC: What sort of movies do you like best?

Major: Well, I saw *King Henry V*. That was very good.

NC: Did you understand it?

Major: Yes. We've just been through the play.

He said he read the newspapers every day, and that he was interested in world affairs. To test this, I asked:

NC: What happened at Nuremberg last week?

Major: Trials. The finals of the Nuremberg trials.

NC: And what was the decision in those trials?

Major: Oh, several of the leading Germans were hanged, three were acquitted. The others got varying terms of imprisonment.

NC: Do you agree with this sentence?

Major: Well . . . (laughs) I don't know, the leading Germans were very clever to be able to twist out of it. I'm not sure about it, I wouldn't pass any opinion.

As in most countries, the United States is known in New Zealand mostly by its movies. This is especially true of youth, and the boys of Rongotai are a case in point. I asked the group:

NC: Who is your favorite actress?

(Boys all laugh)

Major: I wouldn't know the names of them.

NC: Now, that got a big laugh here, and I wonder why. We're going to go around and ask some of your schoolmates who their favorite stars are.

Boy 1: Veronica Lynn. Oh, I mean Veronica Lake.

Boy 2: Greer Garson.

Boy 3: I don't know.

Boy 4: I don't know.

Boy 6: Betty Grable.

Boy 7: Haven't got one.

Boy 8: Joan Leslie.

Boy 9: Rita Hayworth.

Boy 10: Shirley Temple.

NC: Shirley Temple is getting a little old for you now, isn't she?

Boys: (Big laugh)

We interrupted a rugby game when Bland and I arrived with our recording equipment, and it was obvious from the hale condition of these boys, and the fervor with which they played, that sports are as much inbred in the New Zealander as in the Australian or American. I asked the boys what they used as a school cheer and the rugby team went into a huddle to perform a "haka"—a Maori war cry.

The Maori people, whose names and whose hakas the white New Zealander honors by wide usage, has a position of respect and equality enjoyed by few colored minorities anywhere in the English-speaking world. They didn't always have it, and for the better part of a century there was a bitter fighting between them and the settlers.

One of the veterans we spoke to at the rehabilitation center confirmed that today the respect for the Maori is carried well beyond lip service in New Zealand life. Fred Ruhi, a veteran who had fought with distinction in the North African campaign, explained that the government has taken good care of him:

Ruhi: Well, it's given me a trade that I wanted to learn before the war.

NC: They gave you free tuition in carpentry?

Ruhi: Yes, they gave us free tuition and paid us on top of that.

NC: What about housing? Do they help you get located?

Ruhi: Oh, yes, they grant us loans.

NC: The Maori in New Zealand is a minority, isn't he?

Ruhi: Yes.

NC: Do you find that being a minority places you at a disadvantage?

Ruhi: Well, actually no.

NC: You have full rights socially, and every other way, with the New Zealander?

Ruhi: Yes.

NC: There is no discrimination of the Maoris in the schools?

Ruhi: No.

NC: You have mixed classes?

Ruhi: Oh, yes, we have mixed classes.

NC: And there's no discrimination against you in matters of hotel accommodations or traveling, or anything of that order?

Ruhi: No, no.

Mr. Ruhi belongs to a race famous for its courage and chivalry. One of the greatest stories in the history of any warfare concerns a Maori tribe that surrounds a British regiment in a battle of the last century. The Maori chief learned that his enemy was running short of food and ammunition, so he sent a message that his men preferred not to fight on inferior terms. He then sent the British food and ammunition, and both sides took up the fight where they had left off.

But this kind of chivalry was not rewarding, and life became very difficult for Mr. Ruhi's fathers. At one time, 50 years ago, the race was dying. Wars, the diseases of the white man, and broken spirits, had reduced the people from a quarter of a million to a mere 40,000. But when New Zealand's governments became increasingly progressive, the status of the Maori, as well as of the white man, improved. Today, with equal rights, including no discrimination against mixed marriage, he numbers almost 100,000; he holds property; he is represented in government.

I looked up a Maori member of the cabinet—big, white-haired, handsome E. T. Terektane, Minister of Native Affairs. I asked him whether Maoris had full educational rights: "Very much. The right to receive the same standard of education in our schools, such as attending university, with a view of becoming masters in the principles of professions."

From the standpoint of absolute racial harmony, it would be overstating the case to say that New Zealand is perfect in this respect. There was a certain amount of patronizing that I was aware of, as typified by this comment from a man on the street:

"We have a high type of man in the Maori. He is perhaps the most wonderful gentleman, left to himself, that I have ever seen."

In few countries in the world today can you stop a person at random in the street and get from him, or her, an admission of having no worries about economics. Yet many of the people we stopped said that very thing. A young newspaperman told us he was a happy citizen with no worries about his family income. A young woman who worked as a draughtsman in a civil engineering firm explained that she had no money worries, was perfectly solvent, and had plenty of leisure time. A retired grocer also said he had no complaints.

New Zealand is the healthiest country in the world. It has the lowest infant mortality rate and the highest life expectancy. The latter takes tangible form even for the casual visitor. Owen Gillespie, aged 70-plus, is an active member of the prime minister's staff. He ran us ragged showing us splendid state housing projects. Part of this visit included having tea with Gillespie's 91-year old uncle, who spoke of taking a trip to New York one of these days.

The mild climate of the islands has a good deal to do with the health of New Zealanders, but certainly the elaborate program of the government is no small contribution. If a man is ill, he goes to his own doctor—to any doctor of his choosing—and pays a standard fee of 10½ shillings, or about $1.50. He can pay more if he wants, of course. No law against that. He signs a form and the doctor sends it to the government, and the patient gets a refund of 7½ shillings, so that the visit costs him only 3 shillings, or about 45 cents.

If the physician prescribes medicine, the patient takes his prescription to the pharmacy and gets it filled free of charge, the druggist being reimbursed by the government. Any person is entitled to free hospitalization at any time. Mothers are paid a subsidy for each child under a certain age, not as an inducement to have children, but just so the family will be better off.

I asked a housewife named Mrs. Jeffries, mother of five children, how the government had looked after her:

Mrs. Jeffries: Well, the maternity benefits you get are marvelous. When my first children were born, we paid five or six guineas per week in an obstetric hospital and we paid the doctor five guineas a week for his attention. [A New Zealand guinea came to about $3.50 in American money, so she was speaking of expenses totaling about $40 per week.] And when my last children were born, the social security benefits covered all the expenses, and took away all that anxiety the parents might have in looking forward to what should be the happiest event in one's life.

NC: Well, now, this care and the benefits from the government begin prenatally, and go right through the arrival of the child?

Mrs. Jeffries: Yes. They do. You go to your doctor immediately when you know that a baby is to arrive and you visit your doctor regularly every month until the last of the period and then you visit him weekly. My doctor visited me every day while I was in the hospital, and all that didn't cost me at all. That was all covered by social security.

The health regime of the government had the support of a wide majority of the people, but among physicians it was a subject for debate. Some doctors, those hostile to the principle of socialized medicine, we strongly opposed to it; other just as stoutly defended it. We spoke to representatives of both camps.

Dr. H.B. Ewen of Wellington objected to the amount of red tape involved in submitting data to the government:

It (filling out forms) takes up a lot of time, the doctor's time, the patient's time, and when one is busy as one has been, especially during the war years, it became very, very irksome to put up with all this business, see? And of course the whole thing really boils down to this: that the government wants to dictate to doctors and bring them under their thumb.

On the other hand, Dr. Jack of Auckland felt the process was not problematic:

I find it's a very simple matter to obtain the signature on the
form, and once every two weeks to submit these to the health
department. There's very little red tape. There's much less red
tape than there was previously in trying to recover fees. (The doctor) is undoubtedly better off under the present circumstances.

Whatever the merits of its health program, New Zealand is
busy with problems of housing, and too much soil erosion, and
too little waterpower. It's taking steps to cope with these, but it
also has an eye on bigger problems—the problems of a world that
twice in 50 years got itself into a mess ultimately costing the lives
of New Zealanders. Their casualties in the last war were proportionately *four* times greater than our own.

The world and its affairs are not new for the people of this
country. Twelve years ago, the government of New Zealand was
alone among the English-speaking nations in taking a positive
stand for collective security and in calling for aid to the victims
of fascist aggression. In 1935, six years before Pearl Harbor, New
Zealand banned the export of scrap iron to Japan. At Geneva its
spokesman urged the League of Nations to unite against the Axis
in Ethiopia, Spain, and China before it was too late. Today New
Zealanders are just as internationally minded as ever, and on the
strength of their knowledge and experience they were inclined
to share the Australian view that war scares and talk of inevitable
conflict were unjustified and inflammatory.

We visited the Prime Minister of New Zealand, Peter Fraser, in
his office in the Parliament Building. He was working late; it was
past midnight. He told us that the entire parliament and cabinet
very often put in such hours. Fraser, a Scotsman, has an appeal-
ing homeliness about him—a big nose and small, friendly eyes,
and schoolteacher-type specs. He reminded me of one of Disney's
dwarfs in *Snow White*. He told us:

I think that those talks about the inevitability of war are doing
a great deal of harm. I believe it would be possible to have a
peace pact for 50 or 100 years with all the countries of the world,
if the proper spirit were shown. I don't think any responsible

person in the world wants war. There are different opinions in New Zealand as in other countries; but those of us who belong to what we call the progressive side in politics and in outlook on international affairs, certainly look at matters more clearly, and with more single-mindedness.

Just then, there was a ringing bell outside the Prime Minister's office indicating that the House was ready to put an issue to a vote. Mr. Fraser responded with the alertness of a fireman answering an alarm. We left the Parliament House at 1:00 in the morning, and the government was still at work. Symbolically, perhaps, in view of the fact that all New Zealand seemed to be gainfully employed. The week we were there, official figures showed that out of a population of 1,600,000 only 138 people were without jobs. The Minister of Internal Affairs explained to me almost apologetically that some of the 138 were in regions remote from employment opportunities and others were physically handicapped.

As I was about to leave New Zealand I was given a book entitled *Introduction to New Zealand.* Its foreword seemed to me to sum up the character of the dominion:

> New Zealand is a democracy with all the question marks of a democracy. It is independent. It has party conflicts. It assails itself. It admires itself. It tries to learn through experience. It is the usual bundle of contradictions that make up a democratic society. It has a certain unity. We don't want to seem conceited; but we don't want to be too absurdly humble either. We think our country is beautiful and interesting.

I thought so too. And I thought, moreover, that the experiment of this "beautiful and interesting" little democracy is one the world might well watch and study. For New Zealand is boldly attempting to reconcile the best features of private enterprise and socialism, and to eliminate the worst of each. From the standpoint of a traveler looking for signs of harmony between these two great poles of world economy, this was a country important out of all proportion to its size. I had not seen many places where people were free, busy, healthy, unworried, and at one with their minorities. I had not seen many places where children were strong, well fed, well clothed, well housed, well educated, and happy. [In the November 1946, after 14 years of a Labor party, socialist-leaning government, the free-enterprise Nationalists won a majority in the New Zealand House of Representatives in a surprise upset.]

The day before my One World trip was to come to an official close, I was taken to a local movie house to see myself in the newsreel filmed in Sydney. It was better than I thought it would be, less startling and discouraging to me than I expected. But I found out that my lower lip does most of the talking, that my moustache photographs very black, and that I waggle my head more than is necessary. On that last day in the country I was also touched when presented with a lapel pin signifying honorary membership in the New Zealand Air Force Association.

In the morning, the alarm got us up at 5:00. I whisked through a shower, a shave, an egg, and a cup of tea, and we were off in a bus by 5:30. But I forgot my wristwatch, and dashed back in a taxicab to retrieve it. The bus, luckily for me, stopped to pick up additional passengers at a café. So I made it in good time without a hitch. I took my seat at the tail on a comfortable Skymaster and settled down to catching up on my diary. The ride was smooth as a baby's behind.

13

Hawaii, Hollywood, Home

*Sat in the sun on the porch, + felt
the Fatigue ooze out of my pores.*

Fiji was a stop on our way to Hawaii. We were traveling due east, which foreshortened the daylight, and by the time we were over the island it was quite dark. As we descended, we could see small fires of sugar cane being deliberately cleared. But there was no light of any other kind. It was enervating to fly for a whole half hour over the landing area in pitch darkness—but our pilot was doing a "check run" on instrument approaches and this caused the delay. We made a fair landing a few minutes after 7 p.m.

Jerry O'Donnell of Pan Am was there to greet us; also Jerry Adams, attached to the British government public relations office. After a good dinner, we droved 15 miles to what I expected would be a native town, but instead it was Adams' house. Pleasant enough, too. The palms were silhouetted in the brilliance of the full moon lately risen and the night sounds mixed with the faint sound of surf. With us were O'Donnell and Ann Wither, a tall, blonde, wholesome hostess. We had a fairly jolly hour, considering the fatigue, and drove back to the airport.

I went to bed by 11:00, greatly exhausted and stale in the head, still I had to take two ¾-grain Seconals to knock myself out. The sleeping was in a barracks, on an army cot. The night was warm, with a fine cool breeze intermittently rattling through the barracks. Considering that a half dozen men were sleeping in a row of cots, the snore ratio was remarkably small.

The morning dawned as October 13, but within an hour's flight from Nandi, we were back into October 12, having picked up the day at 180-degrees. We had breakfast at the officer's mess, called Fiji Macambo, and then I strolled around the airbase. I took some photographs with Fijians, who are a most pleasant and handsome people. We took off promptly at 8:00 and flew over other islands in the Fiji group. In spite of the short sleep, I felt quite well and put the hours to good use typing several letters.

Right on schedule, we sighted Canton Atoll, sitting by itself in the immense Pacific. The afternoon was clear, the light was sharp, and from our approaching elevation of about 2,000 feet one could pick out every last feature of the atoll.

The captain again made an instrument landing, which took 20 minutes longer. As soon as we disembarked, I wandered away from the crowd, walked down to a beach and peeled off all but my shorts, to catch a little of the afternoon sun. Thirty minutes of this and then dinner.

We were received cordially by the Pan Am men, one of whom knew my work and asked for an autograph. I took advantage of the opening and asked whether it might be possible to sneak in a little fishing before it got dark. It was quickly arranged, and together with Fred Scobey of Pan Am, our pilot Captain George, stewardess Ann Miller, Lee, a British colonel, and two native boys, we pushed off in a bare navy launch and putted out into the ocean.

The tide was coming in and racing furiously around a point. We cruised up and down the western shore of the atoll, trolling spinners and watching the amazing fish life all around us. Marlins and alva were leaping right out of the water—always out of reach, it seemed—and for the first 20 minutes nobody caught a fish. Then they started biting, and at one time three alva were hauled aboard simultaneously. Even I caught one.

There was a flamboyant sunset, and night fell rapidly. We raced for shore and tied up at our dock with barely a single degree of vision left to us. At 9:00 we hit our cots in shack #9, one of about

a 100 such shacks spread along the airstrip. It was warm enough
to need no covering, and we were tired enough to sleep soundly,
were it not for the conversation of two fellow passengers, one of
whom smoked in bed and kept spitting grains of tobacco—"tpt—
tpt—tpt." And then at 10, a torrential rain fell. At 10:15, a south-
bound Pan Am clipper landed right next to us, her four engines
sounding like the eruption of Krakatoa.

We were up at 2:20—a.m.—for a breakfast of wheatcakes.
There was a soft, warm wind blowing—no trace of the heavy
rains—and a clear sky. We took off promptly as scheduled at 4 a.m.
I snoozed for half hour or so, and awoke to see dawn breaking
redly, in a setting of small scattered clouds that stood hard and
blue-black against the eastern sky. Mrs. Buchan, the garrulous
Australian women who sat at my left since Auckland, was admiring
the effect more loudly than was proper in view of the fact that
the cabin was asleep, and when I shushed her, pointing to the
sleepers, she snorted, "It will do them *good* to wake up and see the
wonder of God's world!"

The morning wore on, and with strange relativity. It felt like
4 p.m. at one time and I looked at my watch to see "10:15"—a.m.
I read a bit and typed some letters, and about 90 minutes out of
Honolulu I went up to the cockpit with Captain George and listened
to the technical explanations. He invited me to shoot the sun on
a bubble sextant, an automatic affair that does the basic computa-
tion itself. I managed to keep the image of the sun centered in the
bubble, and my reading, according to a later calculation, was only
5 minutes off.

My first impression of Honolulu from the air was its striking resemblance to Southern California. We landed at Hickam
Field with dispatch and were quickly cleared through customs. A
reporter from the *Star-Bulletin* and a gal from Pan Am's publicity
department were on hand to interview me. Wesley Edwards met us
after a while and we drove to his home beyond Diamond Head.

I phoned Ma & Pa on a poor circuit, also [Corwin's brother]
Emil. I tried unsuccessfully to nap, got up after an hour, and
dined at the Surf Club with the Edwards and another couple.

Loretta Young and her husband Tom Lewis were there with Duke Whoozis, an anonymous swimmer, and I got a short, sharp wake of the nausea of Hollywood society. Lee decided to go on to San Francisco and got a 10 p.m. flight.

The next day I was driven by a Navy yeoman to Pearl Harbor, where for two hours I looked over the vast, busy, buzzing naval installation—biggest, I supposed, in the world. With a personable young lieutenant from New York, I stood atop a very high control tower, and with powerful binoculars picked out the features of the harbor. That evening, I attended a party for Democratic bigwigs at the home of a prosperous Hawaiian lawyer named Trask. I met the governor of the territory, Ingram Stainback, and a dozen other people; and watched the hula performed both well and badly— the latter by volunteers—and ate a great buffet dinner of chicken and poi and salmon.

Edwards arranged to fly to Hilo the next morning by Navy plane, and at 10:30 a.m. we showed up at the airport and we were ushered aboard a little twin-engined Beechcraft—the kind we flew around Cairo with Sandy McNown. Private Moffatt piloted, and for a while I flew her over and along the coast of Molokai—the leeward coast. Here there are sheer cliffs, clean as though sliced by a cheese knife; and deep valleys—all bright green and very much the Pacific Isle topography of legend and fable.

I was fussing and cursing the Kodak Medalist that Lee left behind in my custody. I made a botch of what I hoped would be a decent photographic record of this last side-trip of the tour. The automatic winding mechanism got jammed, and resisted all rational attempts to unjam it. Not until I wasted 2 or 3 spools did I get it to work.

We continued down the leeward coasts of Lanai and Maui, the islands lying east and south of Oahu. Both were striking in their beauty, though not quite up to the spectacular quality of Molokai. (I listened to the last innings of the last game of the World Series flying between Molokai and Maui.) We landed at the Hilo airport so simply and easily in this little plane, that it seemed less complicated than parking a car.

I was astonished, on alighting, to find that the jacket to my best suit, the brown-check suit I bought at Saks, had a frightful rent in the elbow—it had opened along a seam when I stuck it in the little opening of the cockpit window while taking photos, and the force of the wind at 160 mph, had unraveled it. Fortunately we located an obliging Japanese tailor in Hilo, and within a half hour had it sewed up enough for me to reach the mainland.

The heat in Hilo was humid and oppressive, but we soon left it behind when we started driving toward Volcano House. Low hanging clouds obscured the top of Mauna Loa, and there was a cold drizzle to greet us when we reached our destination—just below 4,000 feet. That evening I went to a talk on vulcanology, and to see an excellent color film of the 1942 eruption on Mauna Loa. For the first time I knew there was such a thing as a lava fountain, the evidence being graphic enough in the shots of lava pouring out of the rifts in the mountains.

The next day I took my accursed Kodak Medalist and went out to wrestle with more film. I went to see Halemaumau, the pit; and Kileauea, the crater. I sat in the sun outside Volcano House and caught up on my notes. The afternoon grew cold and windy, but toward nightfall a great cloud that obscured all but a band of golden light toward west, cast into weird relief the scores of plumes of steam escaping from the vents in the upper and lower reaches of the crater.

As often before when I have started to relax after a great strain, I grew depressed. I had dinner alone and did a spot of reading later, which picked me up—Mark Twain's "Letter from a Recording Angel," as turned up by *Harper's*.

We left Volcano House at 10:00 the next morning and drove leisurely down to Hilo, through intermittent rain belts. At Hilo, I saw evidences of the widespread damage done by the great tsunami of a few months ago—the one that swept down the Pacific after an earthquake in the vicinity of the Aleutians. We had lunch at the temporary and improvised quarters of the Hilo Yacht Club, which had been swept away by the wave. They were now using a former Girl Scout hostel.

We had arranged with Captain Courtney Shands of the Navy to pick us up at the big Hilo Naval airport at 2:00, so we lost no time getting to the field after lunch. Shands, who I learned later was one mean pilot and a hero in carrier warfare, showed up at 2:20, stepped out, said easy-like that he'd like to start back soon: "Got to get back to the office." His little Beechcraft was refueled and we were away. No sooner had we taken off and started west on the northern coast of the island, than Shands handed me the controls. I kept them for almost a half hour while he nonchalantly read a newspaper.

Unlike the flight down, we took the shorter, regular leeward course, which nicked the edges of Maui, Lanai, and Molokai. I was especially interested to see one of the dashboard instruments light up cheerfully as we passed directly over the cone of silence above the Maui radio towers on the tip of the island. Shands was piloting at this point, against a cross wind, but he offered me the wheel once again and I added another 10 minutes to my flying time. One or two more junkets and I will have flown for an hour!

Boiling black rain clouds covered the hills behind Honolulu, though hardly any rain was falling on the city itself. The crowning touch on this lush scene was a rainbow that, set against the dark storm clouds, stood vivid and clear, its ultra-violet band being sharper than any I have ever seen. Between the airport and Web's house, I stopped to pick up a bundle of my laundry and then I took a quick shower and finished packing, all in a hurry and a sweat to be on time for a cocktail party in my honor at the sumptuous hillside home of the Hendersons.

The guest included radio people, the theatre and drama league, university people, the governor and Mrs. Stainbeck, Helen [wife of Bill] Costello, Nancy Corbett, Joel Trapido, Mrs. Lawson, and others whose names I either half-heard or forgot. I was lionized, lei'd upon, and smacked for two hours or so. Then I went with the Edwardses and Helen to Trader Vic's for a decent Chinese meal.

I made it to the airport in good time. There, Harold Kent, whom I first met in the War Department in Washington, came up and introduced himself. He said he was now living in Hawaii and introduced a busload of native Islanders who, at Harold's insistence, serenaded me. They had come with guitars and leis to welcome Mrs. Kent, due in on a Constellation not long after our departure. When I boarded the 11:45 flight from Honolulu to Los Angeles, I lost no time rigging up a berth and stretching out. I was lucky enough to have nobody sitting next to me. To my surprise, I fell sound asleep shortly after midnight, and when I next looked at my watch it was 3:00. I tried to sleep again and half-dozed until light began to break in the east. I sat up to watch by pressing my nose to the window and looking backward. I could clearly see the night retreating in full force behind us.

We had breakfast at 6:00 by the Hawaiian time still on my watch. It was a treat—pineapple, orange juice, and peaches. I read, shaved, and wrote a few notes as the afternoon wore on. We made our landfall slightly south of Santa Barbara, flying in over the islands of San Miguel, Santa Rosa, Santa Cruz, and the Anacapas. There was a haze over the mainland, and we couldn't plainly see the Santa Ynez Mountains, but soon we edged in toward the coast, and I could plainly identify the coastal highway, Malibu, and the principal canyons.

Down the coast we went, and turned into the depression at Santa Monica, flying right over the Palisades and [Charles] Laughton's house, then cutting across Beverly Hills and over Em's [Corwin's brother Emil's] house on Vista Grande, across the Hollywood Hills, a long loop around Burbank, and a perfect landing.

Photographers and reporters were there—and Em and my sister-in-law Freda, Chuck Lewin and his wife Bobby, Broadway producer Ernie Martin, CBS director Bill Robson, and Harry Witt. I was bedraggled and considerably out of press, having lived and traveled in one suit since leaving New Zealand. I answered a few questions put by a *Daily News* reporter—mainly regarding Russia, and then went off to Em's for dinner. Then it was home to the Harburgs and bed by 11:00. [Corwin stayed with E. Y. "Yip" Harburg, the great American lyricist, author of "Brother, Can You Spare a Dime?" and the complete collection of songs in *The Wizard of Oz.*]

The next day, I sat in the sun on the porch and felt the fatigue ooze out of my pores. In the evening there was a houseful of people at the Harburgs to see *The True Glory*. Foolishly, I stayed up talking until nearly 4 a.m. I loafed all day the next day too, but late in the afternoon I drove out to Santa Monica to see playwright Don Stewart and his wife Ella Winters, Ira and Mrs. Wolfert, and Mrs. Berthold Brecht. They pumped me full of questions about the trip, urged me to report to Truman. When I said I'd be glad to do so, but not without an invitation, Ella spoke to Helen Fuller in Washington and asked her to set it up. She later inscribed and presented me with a copy of her book, *I Saw the Russian People*.

I continued my rest regime the following day—slept late, lay in the sun for a couple hours, but I did get a little bat-swinging exercise. For the first time in months, I did absolutely nothing all day and all night—not even going out on either of two dates that presented themselves most attractively. Instead, I took my weary bones to bed early.

Eventually, I had to get to work on the piece on my One World trip that I'd promised *McCall's* magazine. In the evening, I told a roomful people at the Harburgs—people who had been carefully selected and invited to hear me give a confidential report on the trip. The group included Em and Freda, Charles Laughton, Keenan Wynn, Joan Loring, Ona Munson, the Gombergs, Hy Kraft, Kay Swift, and Larry Merill. I talked longer than I intended, but held their interest. Late-stayers included Ona, who kept us up until 3 a.m.

Tired and dopey from the previous night's exertions, I spent most of the day in the garden. But at 5 p.m., I left for a fundraising cocktail party for Henry Wallace at Ciro's. I stayed for his speech and then went to pick up Joan Loring; we had dinner at Chasen's. We went to Em's afterward for some first-class card tricks. Then I took Joan home and didn't get back until 3 a.m. [Henry A. Wallace was FDR's running mate in 1940 and served as vice president from 1941 to 1945. In 1946, he was deliberating a run for the presidency in 1948 as a Progressive Party candidate.]

When I'd met Wallace at the party, he asked whether I could meet him at the Biltmore in downtown Los Angeles at 7:00 the next morning. As this would mean rising at 5:30, I turned it down, and thought that would be the end of it. But at 10:30, I was awakened by a phone call from Wallace's right-hand man, David Karr, and a meeting was set up for 12:30 at a political club on Central Avenue. I drove through heavy traffic to the 4000s on Central, to find nothing resembling a political club. So I raced to Burbank, where I knew Wallace would be emplaning sometime that afternoon.

I tried in vain to find out exactly when he was due, and succeeded only when an American Airlines girl, Mitzi Dabardis, confronted me with a picture of myself, which she had been carrying in her wallet. "Is this you?" she asked. "I *thought* you'd show up here *sometime*," she said, "If I waited long enough." Mitzi came to my rescue, although not before the local FBI, suspicions aroused by my inquiries after Wallace, started watching me.

Wallace and Karr showed up about 20 minutes before the plane's departure, and Wallace and I spoke for a while on the benches outside the waiting room. Karr urged me to fly to San Diego with Wallace, as it was only an hour distant. I took it on.

Tired from his travels, and suffering from a cold, Wallace listened at first spiritlessly to my account of what I'd seen, but he picked up at moments. I told him about Czechoslovakia and China, MacArthur and Japan, my stay in Russia, my impressions of Manila, Australia and New Zealand. At moments he appeared shocked and depressed when I added fact to fact. He found my report a general corroboration and extension of his own information. He opened a briefcase and pulled out some letters he had received from informed sources, some formerly OSS personnel, describing the situation in Romania, for one country. The gist and main point of this confidential information was that U.S. diplomatic and military personnel were fraternizing with anti-democratic elements almost *entirely*.

I told Wallace of the reaction to his Garden speech as I observed it in Manila, Australia and New Zealand; then went on to say that I thought he had knocked the reactionaries off balance with his speech and letter. I said that it was important, in my view, to keep punching and punching hard; that he was the last and best bulwark against the rising fascism in this country; the best guarantee of survival of civil liberties and true democratic freedom. I asked him also whether he thought his new post with the *New Republic* was big enough for him. He said he thought so; that it left him free to travel and speak; that the magazine had big plans for expansion.

We landed at dusk and I could barely glimpse the city and the harbor with all its shipping as we were approaching the airport. Wallace was met by the press and local Democrats. He was whisked off after we said goodbye. But David Karr stayed behind at the airport and we discussed Wallace, his future, his techniques of speaking, and Democratic Party strategy, and columnist Drew Pearson (for whom Karr worked) until it was time for my plane to leave.

The night was mild—a good thing since I had no hat or coat. I boarded a Western Airlines Skymaster at 6:00 and flew north to Burbank. When we arrived, I picked up my car at the parking lot and drove to Em's for dinner. The next day I spent the morning and forenoon sunning, the afternoon entertaining Jeanne Meredith, the early evening with Em and Freda, and the late evening packing my stuff. Soon I was on a crowded American Airlines flight that left a few minutes before midnight. I slept until I was awakened as we approached Tulsa.

On the flight from Tulsa to Chicago, a young dentist from California had the seat next to me, and as it was his first flight, I invited him to sit next to the window, swapping places. The flight was smooth and fast, with a tailwind, and we arrived early. However, trouble developed with the brakes on takeoff, and we were delayed a whole hour. On this last lap I alternated between reading, resting, and talking politics with my dentist friend.

When we arrived at LaGuardia, I was met by about 20 reporters and cameramen, and a group of family and friends. My brother Al drove us home in my car, and as soon as we were established in the door of 38 Central Park South, I phoned the folks to say that the trip was over, and that I was safely home.

14

Postscripts to One World

On November 8, 1946 Corwin presented his One World Flight report to the sponsors of the Willkie Award at the Willkie Memorial Building in New York City. A portion of his remarks follows.

Corwin's Conclusions

Whether this mission has succeeded, I am the least able to judge. Its main accomplishments are not yet fully unpacked; indeed not even fully arrived. For, on the way around, between the many formalities of a social and political nature, we managed to record a hundred hours of the voices and opinions of people, big and little, of seventeen countries. These recordings, made on spools of magnetic wire, were sent home by American diplomatic pouch, and so fast was our journeying that we have beaten some of them back. Ultimately they will be heard on the air; and I feel that it will be from these results that the value of the mission can be appraised.

Physically, the dimensions of the trip were these: 37,000 miles, flown on the ships of 19 different commercial and military airlines, in something less than 200 hours. The flight was made under excellent auspices, and we were cordially received everywhere. The great name of Wendell Willkie cast its aura before us. It is not every traveler who can be guided by so pure a spiritual compass.

Now I think it is understood that I am not a diplomat or politician; I have not made a career of reporting from abroad. But I do have eyes and ears, and in the enterprise just concluded I had a recording machine to go along with them. My impressions, the conclusions which have come out of the many miles and hours, are, for whatever they are worth, based upon meetings and events, testimonies, anecdotes, expected and unexpected answers, irritations, evasions, euphemisms and persuasions, the dancing of attendance so I could not see certain things, and, contrariwise, the blunt and candid laying bare of inequities, shortcomings, and injustices. Words were said to me out of the sides of mouths, behind hands, words sometimes dangerous to the people who said them because secret police might be about; also there were false words, false on face value. There was many a sincere toast and many a hollow one; it is all in the record. Here then are an even dozen conclusions:

1. We seem to be farther from Willkie's *One World* today than we were when his thesis became the best-selling book in America four years ago. Everybody is agreed on the desirability of One World, but very few on the method. It was the consensus of my interviews that none of us will get far in any direction if the leading powers of the world fail to set an example, as Mr. Nehru calls upon them to do, by putting our ideals to work; and it was emphasized that the leading powers must begin by cleaning up undemocratic processes and practices at home; that only then can each face the world with clear conscience, and assume its rightful share of responsibility and moral leadership.

2. The reservoir of goodwill toward the United States, about which Willkie spoke enthusiastically in 1942, has drained to a dangerously low level. We are suspected, disliked, resented, and even hated in some of the very countries where Willkie found the greatest appreciation and friendship for us during the war.

3. A powerful and elemental sense of fairness, as well as an overwhelming will and anxiety for peace, pervades all of the peoples of the earth. It was generally felt if the statesmen representing these peoples were more truly and conscientiously

to mirror their views, there would be a much better chance for the compromise necessary to keep the peace and establish a secure world.

4. It seemed to me that the greatest peril today is a sort of Frankensteinian phobia created by factions who would have people everywhere believe there is no room in one world for more than one economic and social system. In view of the existing facts, such a world obviously could not be achieved without a war in which one crushes the other. To me this inevitability would be easier to accept if it were not for the fact that in several of the countries which we visited it was impossible to distinguish whether we were in a world of capitalism or socialism, since patterns were being sought which would blend the best features of both. Hence, it suggests itself that if a united country can base its future on a combination of the most workable essences of opposing systems, we have no right to rule out the possibility that the same can be done by a united world. Indeed, it seems to me that the very basis of a democratically united world is the establishment, first of the will, then of the means, by which differing social and economic systems can live amicably together. And the most important contribution to be made toward this goal is to convince the peoples of the world that a war is not inevitable. This task I consider the first responsibility of the great powers. In the meantime, the worst possible approach from any side is to attempt by propaganda, polemics, intimidation, or by force, to persuade one system to abandon what it considers its righteous course for the other. This, as we have seen in the long history of political and religious warfare, can only widen, not narrow, basic differences.

5. In view of the existing tendency to diplomatic impasse, the principle of mutual compromise must replace the Gibraltar complex in international politics. As Mr. Attlee has suggested, "It is worthwhile to have some idea as to the activities in which we are in agreement." Most of the statesmen I interviewed believe with him that we must lay off exaggerating differences

and making atrocities out of them; that instead we must transfer headline and glamour-appeal to areas of agreement, of which there are more than we are inclined to credit.

6. I believe the democracies of the West should watch with neighborly interest and goodwill, rather than with distrust, the social experimentation of countries like Czechoslovakia and New Zealand, which are trying to reconcile extremes of socialism and private enterprise. We are perhaps lucky that such problems are being worked out by them in laboratory fashion, rather than on the battlefield, as in China. And if their experiments contain anything worthy of emulation by the rest of us, let us take up their best features, just as so much of the world outside America benefited from our experiment with independence; and democracy after the revolution of 1776.

7. One of the most frequently and strongly reiterated impressions of the entire trip was that the United States, in the eyes of the rest of the world, is a colossus without precedent and without peer; that we hold in our hands as does no other nation, the means to keep the world at peace. Whether or not people liked us, they were respectful of our power and our capacity; and they attempted, some of them fearfully, others hopefully, to convince me as a listening American, that peace lies not in our stars, but in us.

8. I believe all nations should acknowledge more readily the principle of cultural exchange, especially as it applies between countries whose political relations are strained. It is pleasant enough to exchange artists and students and new compositions with countries who love us, but cultural exchange takes on its greatest meaning and value in cases where the respective peoples, knowing too little of each other, harbor mutual suspicions and apprehensions.

9. I believe freedom of information is an international must, but, to establish it, we must abrogate freedom of misinformation. Let the radio, press, and cinema of the world, whose

responsibility today is graver than ever before in history, regulate themselves so that misinformation becomes a punishable violation of their own laws. Let the radio and press of the world protect both nations and individuals from defamation or assassination by any old demagogue who arises on a convention floor. Let truth and accuracy head up the copy desk, and give them power of decision over the publisher's or the broadcaster's personal political prejudices.

10. I believe that the world would benefit greatly if two pieces of modern American writing were made compulsory reading in every classroom of the countries of the United Nations: Willkie's *One World,* and Hersey's *Hiroshima,* both of which have the power, continuously and profoundly, to influence our time.

11. I believe, from what I've seen, that to despair of the world is to resign from it. I believe that to assume human nature is committed to another war is to assume that suicide is the only solution to our problems.

12. I have lost no hope. I believe that ultimately we will find unity and brotherhood in this world, but that the quest will go on through terrible trials and agonies, until a true democracy, not merely a lip-service democracy, is achieved for the entire world. I believe each of us can assist in this mammoth task; and by such assistance, honor the memory of the man whose name stands for the greatest challenge of our lives—One World.

Legacies

In the weeks and months following Corwin's summary report, he worked assiduously on the *One World Flight* documentary series. CBS engineers transferred the material on the wire recorder to newly available audiotape. Working from typed transcripts, Corwin mapped out and scripted the programs. The recorded segments selected for inclusion were then transferred to acetate discs to use in production. Each episode was broadcast live, including the musical score by Lyn Murray. Guy Della Cioppa assisted in the direction of the programs while Corwin narrated.

One World Flight premiered on January 14, 1947, and aired each Tuesday evening for the following twelve weeks. The series garnered a good deal of praise, especially for its pioneering use of interviews recorded in the field. *Variety* noted that *One World Flight* "broadened the scope of documentary with actuality sequences, uniting it into a whole with brilliant, pungent commentary."

The audience draw was disappointing, however. The fact that Corwin's series was programmed opposite of Bob Hope's show on NBC was seen by many liberals as a sign that socially conscious broadcasting was losing support at CBS, once the leader in that realm. The national mood was shifting.

In the fall of 1947, there was a pall over Hollywood. An investigation of so-called subversive elements in the film industry was underway by the House Un-American Activities Committee (HUAC). Weeks of closed-door testimony culminated with public hearings in Washington, D.C., chaired by Congressman John Parnell Thomas of New Jersey. He was a Republican who held right-wing views, including the belief that FDR and his New Deal policies had "sabotaged the capitalist system."

Behind closed doors, the committee interviewed forty-one people employed in the motion picture industry. They were "friendly witnesses" who volunteered their testimony. The names of nineteen people considered to be Communists or communist sympathizers emerged during the sessions. Those "hostile witnesses" who refused to testify in the public hearings became known as the Hollywood Ten.

Corwin joined with a group of other show business notables who believed a genuine threat to free expression was unfolding. They dubbed themselves the Committee for the First Amendment—and radio was their first tool of resistance. The week after the public hearings began, the program *Hollywood Fights Back* aired on the ABC network. With Corwin producing the primary segment from Hollywood and William Robson directing in New York, a cavalcade of movie stars on both coasts made their case. Among them were Humphrey Bogart, Charles Boyer, Eddie Cantor, Joseph Cotten, Ava Gardner, John Garfield, Danny Kaye, Gene Kelly, Burt Lancaster, Peter Lorre, Frederic March, Vincent Price, Margaret Sullavan, and Robert Young.

One of the participants took to the microphone and said,

> This is Judy Garland. Have you been to a movie this week? Are you going to a movie tonight, or maybe tomorrow? Look around the room. Are there any newspapers lying on the floor, any magazines on your table, any books on your shelves? It has always been your right to read or see anything you wanted to. But now it seems to be getting kind of complicated.
>
> For the past week in Washington, the Thomas-Rankin House Committee on Un-American Activities has been investigating the film industry. I have never been a member of a political organization, but have been following the investigation—and I don't like it.
>
> There are lots of stars here to speak to you. We're in show business, yes, but we're also American citizens. It's one thing if someone says we're not good actors; that hurts, but we can take it. Something else again to say we're not good Americans.

Frank Sinatra warned,

> Once they get the movies throttled, how long will it be before the Committee goes to work on the freedom of the air? How long will it be before we will be told what we can or cannot say into a radio microphone? If you make a pitch on nationwide network for a square deal for the underdog, will they call you a commie? Will we have to think Mr. Rankin's way to get into the elevator at Radio City? Are they going to scare us into silence? I wonder. If this Committee gets a green light from the American people now, will it be possible to make a broadcast like this a year from today?

There was an ironic twist in the HUAC story. Syndicated columnist Drew Pearson, who had been critical of Representative

Thomas's methods, received documents from the congressman's secretary revealing that Thomas had corruptly padded his government office payroll. When summoned before a grand jury, Thomas invoked the Constitutional protection that he had refused to afford the Hollywood Ten. He was tried and convicted of fraud. Thomas served his eighteen-month sentence in Danbury Prison, where screenwriters Lester Cole and Ring Lardner Jr. were incarcerated on contempt of court charges stemming from their refusal to answer Thomas's questions.

Hollywood Fights Back might have temporarily slowed the steamroller, but not for long. The investigation into "un-American" activities would soon grow to be a full-fledged witch-hunt—and Corwin would be caught in the wider net being cast in the national obsession against communism. CBS received a HUAC request for the *One World Flight* scripts.

In the summer of 1948, Corwin was on his way to New York aboard the *Sante Fe Chief*. It so happened that CBS president William Paley and his wife were on the same train. Corwin and Paley had lunch together in the dining car on the second day of the journey. They talked about the future of CBS and about Corwin's career in radio.

Paley broached the subject of the importance of programming with mass appeal as the business of broadcasting was getting more competitive. Corwin had a "special audience," he said. "We've simply got to face up to the fact that we're a commercial business." Corwin interpreted the conversation to mean, "We'd like you to join the cattle drive for listeners, and this means lowering your standards." Corwin knew his time at CBS was drawing to a close, as well his hopes to form a special unit to produce documentaries. This was confirmed when his next contract with the network offered terms so unacceptable that he could only conclude that it was designed for him to turn down.

In March 1949, Corwin took a position, created specifically for him, as chief of special projects for United Nations Radio. Three months later, he was stunned to learn that the FBI had falsely accused him of being a communist sympathizer and "fellow traveler" based on information from "Confidential Informant ND 336." In fact, Corwin had been under surveillance since 1947 when the communist newspaper *The Daily Worker* had praised *One World Flight*. The modus operandi of Red Scare investigations depended on the betrayal of an honored principle in American justice—the right to face one's accuser.

While many others who were tainted by their appearance on smear lists could not find work and suffered great personal harm, Corwin continued in his position at UN Radio and created some of his best and most highly creative work for the medium. His plays, including *Citizen of the World, Could Be*, and *Document A/777*, mined the *One World* themes that were growing increasingly out of fashion in government circles.

Democratic Senator Pat McCarran of Nevada criticized the United Nations on the floor of Congress for hiring to high positions individuals "directly from the fields of subversive activity." "Mr. Corwin," he said, "is cited as a Communist and subversive by the Attorney General of the United States. Mr. Corwin is or has been a member of a long list of Communist-front organizations."

"McCarran," Corwin countered, "is a political mad dog who wrote admiringly of his friend, [Spain's] dictator Francisco Franco, a comrade of Hitler and Mussolini."

Throughout the late 1940s, an organization called American Business Consultants, made up of three former FBI agents, published *Counterattack*, a newsletter of "facts to combat Communism." It was typically a few pages long. But in June 1950, a special 241-page edition titled *Red Channels: The Report of Communist Influence in Radio and Television* was published and sold out quickly for $1.00 per copy.

It had been an informal practice by Hollywood studios since the start of the HUAC investigations to offer pledges that employment would not be knowingly given to suspected Communists or disloyal Americans. *Red Channels* served to formalize the process in broadcasting by providing a neat list for networks and producers to consult. About it the preeminent media historian of the twentieth century, Erik Barnouw, has written,

The list was enough to bring gasps. Advance hints from *Counterattack* and columnists had made the industry expect revelations of insidious underground activity. What they received was a list of 151 of the most talented and admired people in the industry— mostly writers, directors, performers. They were people who had helped make radio an honored medium, and who were becoming active in television. Many had played a prominent role in wartime radio, and had been articulators of American war aims. In short it was a roll of honor.

Corwin, fittingly, was among those listed. Decades later, he reflected on the meaning:

> The blacklist was the iron curtain of the worst kind, impenetrable for most people. In my case the economic impact was felt, but not gravely. I frequently experienced unexpected, inexplicable stalemates in professional negotiations, but I wrote a book during that period and worked on some films. I did have revenue. The main impact was on my spirit. I grieved for America. I felt a betrayal of all the principles that libertarian America had evolved and defended over the years—Jefferson through Lincoln, Emerson through Whitman to Sandburg. I numbered my plays among those of a broad segment of American thought and culture, and the blacklist demonstrated how one's plays can be writ in water, can fail to reinforce even those who commissioned them—the networks. Our spirit of liberalism had been as ruthlessly suppressed as anywhere in the world, short of the kind of torture and murder that you find in truly benighted countries. That swing to the right was pronounced, long lasting, and devastating.
>
> The 1950s were an awful decade. There were people who were heroes to me dropping by the wayside, exiled, punished, jailed, ostracized. And there was the death of my medium. I had been riding a wonderful charger—a beautiful horse, the saddle and equipage of which was furnished by a great network—and that horse was shot out from under me. I suffered along with all the other serious radio artists.

When television eclipsed radio as the dominant medium in American life, Norman Corwin entered the second phase of his career as an artist, public intellectual, civil thinker, and—always—unapologetic liberal. Among the highlights of his astonishing body of work in the second half of the twentieth century, and well into the twenty-first, are his Academy Award-nominated script for the 1956 film biography of Vincent van Gogh, *Lust for Life*; the stage play *The Rivalry*, about the Lincoln-Douglas Debates, which opened on Broadway in 1959 and was revived in 2008 with Paul Giamati as Stephen Douglas and David Straithairn as Abe Lincoln; *The World of Carl Sandburg*, a portrayal of the poet's life through selected works adapted for stage, which reached Broadway in 1960 with Bette Davis as a lead performer; several TV documentaries in the early 1960s, including two programs for the series FDR that aired on ABC in 1963; the 1970 anthology TV series *Norman Corwin Presents*, produced for Westinghouse Broadcasting; books of poetry, including *Overkill and Megalove* (1963), *Prayer for the 1970s* (1972), *Jerusalem Printout* (1972), and *Network at Fifty* (1976); the stage play *Together Tonight! Jefferson, Hamilton, and Burr*, which toured the country during the bicentennial year 1976; books of social commentary, including *Holes in a Stained Glass Window* (1978) and *Trivializing America* (1984); several major broadcasts for public radio, including, *We Hold These Truths* 1991, a celebration of the 200th anniversary of the Bill of Rights; *Our Lady of the Freedoms* (1997), which traces the history of the Statue of Liberty; *The Writer with the Lame Left Hand* (1997), in commemoration of the 450th anniversary of the birth of Miguel de Cervantes; and *Memos to a New Millennium*, narrated by Walter Cronkite and broadcast on December 31, 1999. Corwin never coasts.

As this is written, Norman Corwin approaches his centenary. Those who love him hope that he derives great delight in the secure knowledge that his work endures and continues to inspire. Much of what Corwin has created since the mid-twentieth century is compelling and humane because of his One World Flight insights and epiphanies. The revisiting of the journey is not just about history; Norman Corwin's thoughts and observations hold lessons that still have practical applications if a serious quest for global harmony is ever on the international agenda. Playwright Jerome Lawrence, in his contemporaneous review of *One World Flight* for *Hollywood Quarterly*, provides an apt sentiment for use at this juncture: "It was good to send a poet around the world. He has a way of listening to the rhythms of tomorrow."

Index